TRIUMPH
B O O K S

TAKE YOUR EYE OFF THE PUCK

TAKE YOUR EYE OFF THE PUCK

HOW TO WATCH HOCKEY
BY KNOWING WHERE TO LOOK

GREG WYSHYNSKI

TRIUMPH
BOOKS

Library of Congress Catalging-in-Publication Data

Wyshynski, Greg, 1977–
  Take your eye off the puck : how to watch hockey by knowing where to look / Greg Wyshynski.
    pages cm
  ISBN 978-1-62937-120-7
1. Hockey. I. Title. II. Title: Hockey.
  GV847.W97 2015
  796.962—dc23

                              2015022554

This book is available in quantity at special discounts for your group or organization. For further information, contact:

Triumph Books LLC
814 N. Franklin
Chicago, Illinois 60610
(312) 337-0747
www.triumphbooks.com

Printed in U.S.A.
ISBN: 978-1-62937-120-7
Design by Paul Petrowsky
Graphics and illustrations by Andy Hansen unless otherwise indicated
Page production by Patricia Frey
Title page photo courtesy of Getty Images

To the puckheads, the fanatics, the rink rats, and anyone who ever shed a tear over this stupid, silly game of ours. Remember, there's no such thing as a non-hockey fan; only those who have yet to let the light of hockey shine unto their hearts...

Is hockey hard? I don't know, you tell me. We need to have the strength and power of a football player, the stamina of a marathon runner, and the concentration of a brain surgeon. But we need to put all this together while moving at high speeds on a cold and slippery surface while five other guys use clubs to try and kill us. Oh yeah, did I mention that this whole time we're standing on blades $\frac{1}{8}$ of an inch thick? Is ice hockey hard? I don't know, you tell me. Next question.

—Brendan Shanahan

=CONTENTS=

=FOREWORD=

JEREMY ROENICK

I love my job as an analyst for the NHL on NBC. After playing hockey for most of my life, getting to sit around and talk about the game for a living has made for a pretty nice second career.

The team I get to work with—from Liam McHugh, Keith Jones, Mike Milbury, Kathryn Tappen, and the rest of the on-air talent to the crew and NBC staff—is top of the line and makes our broadcasts entertaining and informative. I know we have a lot of fun on the set, and I think our viewers and fans have fun watching us on TV.

If we had an unlimited amount of time, I'd like nothing more than to talk about the finer points of the game, all the Xs and Os and little plays that make the difference between winning and losing. Unfortunately, we only have a few minutes to recap what's happening before we throw it back to the game action.

That's where a book like *Take Your Eye Off the Puck* comes in.

Hockey fans today know more about the game than they probably ever have, but you can watch 10 NHL games every week and still not fully understand what's going on. All the set plays the coaches draw up, the tricks that veteran players know how to pull, the reasons deflected goals aren't "lucky," and a million other parts of the game can get overlooked if you aren't watching for them.

After reading this book, you'll have a better understanding of how teams put their rosters together, how power plays and penalty kills are organized, how to get the most out of the advanced stats we're starting to collect, and everything else that happens on the ice.

See you at the rink!

=INTRODUCTION=

At 14:43 of the second overtime session in Game 5 of the 2014 Stanley Cup Final, Alec Martinez scored the series-winning goal for the Los Angeles Kings, vanquishing the New York Rangers and giving the City of Angels its second Cup in three years—and in the process earning me a share of the game-winning goal pool, which kept me awash in In-N-Out combo meals for the rest of the weekend.

That's what you remember seeing on TV, right? Rangers goalie Henrik Lundqvist burying his gorgeous face in the blue paint of his crease as sticks flew through the air and the Kings mobbed their overtime hero? The black jersey–clad Orange County natives in the stands, leaping up and down in euphoria, trying not to pop their cosmetic surgery stitches? The Rangers players stoically staring across the empty rink, wondering if they'd ever advance that deeply into the postseason again (perhaps forgetting how hot-knife-through-room-temperature-butter it is to win in the Eastern Conference)?

Nothing in organized sports comes close to the unpredictability of a playoff overtime in the NHL, and the sudden catharsis or agony that accompanies its finale. Nothing in organized sports comes close to what happened next on that June evening in SoCal: the pageantry of Hockey's Holy Grail being bestowed upon its greatest team, as men on the ice become boys on the pond while they raise the Cup to the heavens.

But what makes hockey great is that it's not just a moment of visceral thrills or superficial ecstasy. Everything that happens in the game— every goal, every shot, every shift, every save—are the last dominos to topple over in a strikingly long sequence of events.

It's a player lifting the Cup, with hundreds of invisible arms lifting it with him.

Think of Martinez scoring that goal. He beat Lundqvist to the blocker side, with a gaping net at which to shoot. Pretend you've got this game on your DVR and hit rewind.

As a defenseman, Martinez could have decided to lead the scoring rush out of his own zone, or let the forwards handle it as he hung back. But he skated up with them, giving the Kings a brief odd-man rush before the exhausted Rangers back-checked.

Martinez passed to center Kyle Clifford, who passed to winger Tyler Toffoli, who skated into the attacking zone and unloaded a shot on Lundqvist. Henrik made the save but couldn't angle the rebound to a safe place in the zone, instead sending it to an onrushing Martinez.

Why was Martinez open for the shot? Because defenseman Kevin Klein of the Rangers decided to take Clifford as he drove the net, while both John Moore and Mats Zuccarello decided to defend Toffoli's shot. That left Martinez unmarked for what amounted to a hockey layup.

Dial it back a few more moments: how did the Kings get out of their own zone so quickly and effectively?

Well, the Rangers rushed two forecheckers deep into the attacking zone; Zuccarello, their sniper, was late getting from the neutral zone to the front of the Kings' net. A centering feed by Derick Brassard from Gretzky's Office was intercepted by Matt Greene, who passed the puck to Martinez, and away he went down the ice.

Dial it back even a few more moments: why was Martinez on the ice at that point in the game? Because the Kings' top defensive pairing of Drew Doughty and Jake Muzzin came off on a change, having skated a 50-second shift about a minute earlier. On came Martinez, Greene, and the Kings' fourth line, which coach Darryl Sutter rolled with confidence throughout the postseason, allowing his top scorers some much-needed rest.

OK, now pump up that DVR rewind to unforeseen speeds. Like, well beyond "x4."

Dial it back a few months.

Where did this court of Kings come from? Well, Clifford had anchored the Kings' fourth line since the 2013 postseason. Toffoli was a rookie on the 2013–14 Kings, settling into a role alongside Clifford. Martinez skated with Greene during the Kings' 2012 Stanley Cup season, winning his first ring. He entered 2013–14 in a numbers crunch on the blue line. There was no promise that Martinez would be a regular for the Kings. But he earned his ice time with solid play, and there he was in Game 5.

Your DVR remote should be smoking by now, but who cares? Dial it back a few *years*.

Why was Martinez a King?

He was drafted by the team in the fourth round of the 2007 Entry Draft, No. 95 overall. The Kings needed defensive prospects in their system, and the Michigan-born Miami University (OH) prospect intrigued them. But then the team drafted star Drew Doughty, and three more defensemen, in the following year, so Martinez gestated in the minor leagues until 2010–11, when he played 60 games as a rookie for L.A.

The next season, he was a Stanley Cup champion. Two years later, he was a playoff legend.

What if on that fateful afternoon in 2007, the Kings had opted to draft Cade Fairchild instead—a 19-year-old from Duluth who went No. 96 overall, and played a total of five games in the NHL? What if Martinez never emerged from the pack of other young defensemen? What if Martinez and Greene never clicked, or Clifford and Toffoli?

What if Darryl Sutter hadn't decided to put the energy line out there in double overtime? What if the Kings didn't execute that passing play?

What if the Rangers hadn't gotten their wires crossed on that shift? What if Lundqvist pulled off a miraculous save? What if Martinez had flubbed the shot?

If "ifs" and "buts" were candy and nuts, then hockey would be Willy Wonka.

When a team hoists the Stanley Cup, it's lifting the weight of hundreds of thousands of decisions along with it; decisions made on the ice and off that all led to that moment. One variable changes, and the fate of the team could change with it. It's like the Butterfly Effect—OK, given the sport, maybe the Butterfly (Goalie) Effect.

If you're reading this book, it's because you're curious about those decisions. You're someone who knows that the game goes so far beyond what's captured by that big swinging television camera at center ice. You understand that taking your eye off the puck allows one to fully appreciate every other aspect of hockey and, thus, appreciate where the fickle little biscuit is headed next, and who might be there to stop it.

The NHL is still seen by the non-believers as a crude, brutal, foreign game; where two guys punching each other in the face is more symbolic of the sport's virtues than cerebral athleticism and strategy. This book explains why hockey is actually the perfect marriage of strategy and ingenuity; of preparation and improvisation; and of wisdom and will.

Why every position played and decision made is a product of history, savvy, and instinct.

Why taking your eye off the puck means opening your eyes to the beautiful nuance of hockey.

And, on occasion, to two guys punching each other in the face because they're paid to do so. What a life.

CHAPTER 1

WHAT THE HECK IS GOING ON OUT THERE?

You know what I love about hockey? The speed.

Not just the speed of the skaters, who can glide as fast as 30 mph for the fastest of them. It's the movement of 10 bodies on the ice, the ones coming off the bench, the chasing of the puck to all corners of the rink, and how it all resets in an instant depending on who earns possession, like birds flying in formation.

Baseball, by comparison? Like watching a slug crawl across flypaper. Basketball, by comparison? Like watching a hockey game made up of 250 24-second power plays and penalty kills…except you only have to watch the last four minutes of each game to feel fulfilled. Football, by comparison? Physicality, frequent changing of personnel…but a game flow that resembles a clogged ketchup nozzle.

Anyone who has watched a hockey game with two teams trading chances for several minutes knows what's up: there's nothing that approaches the velocity, synchronicity, and unpredictability of the sport. It's controlled chaos at times, machine-like precision at others.

This is something that you can only experience in the arena. (Or the stadium, depending on how much cash the NHL decides on grabbing in a given season with its outdoor games.) Television, given the current tech and its limitations, can't convey everything that makes live hockey so exhilarating.

Case in point: they never have to make the puck glow in the arena so you can locate it. Or give it a comet tail.

For years, I've proffered the theory that there aren't "people who don't like hockey," but rather people who have yet to let the light of hockey into their hearts. And the best way to bring these heathens to our religion of choice is to get them to one of our frozen temples and watch a game live.

But once they get there, they might ask: what the heck is going on?

DOING LINES

For decades, the basic setup of a team's forward group has remained static. You have:

The First Line—This is home to your best offensive skill players, the group that's supposed to give opponents fits. Stars, captains, creatures of ego. Usually a Canadian or two. (18-21 minutes in time on ice)

The Second Line—Also home to dynamic offensive players, but frequently ones who can play well defensively, too. Coaches won't hesitate to go power vs. power by putting this group out against another team's top line, because this can be where the team's best defensive center can be found, such as Boston's Patrice Bergeron. It's called the "Second Line" in honor of the time it takes for fans to argue that it's actually the first line based on the stats. (18-21 minutes in time on ice)

The Third Line—This is the traditional "checking line," playing against one of the opponent's top two lines. Here is where you'll find centers who are faceoff specialists and wingers who grind like Miley Cyrus— one of whom is usually a solid scorer who doesn't fit into the top six, but picks up the trash left behind by his tenacious linemates. (14-17 minutes in time on ice)

The Fourth Line—Your home for muckers, meatheads, and misanthropes. This is the "energy line" that features checking pests and brawlers, whose task is to cry havoc, let slip the dogs of war, and collect penalty minutes. But for all the circus music they can orchestrate, a strong fourth line can frequently be an X-factor in a given playoff series. (6-11 minutes of ice time)

Teams roll three defensive pairings, which stack up thusly:

The First Pairing—Your best two-way, stud defenseman, capable of eating up minutes, shutting down foes, and contributing to the offense. Sometimes paired with the team's second-best defenseman; more often paired with a defenseman who makes up for his shortcomings, e.g., a stay-at-home player to help the offensively active star defenseman. (22-26 minutes of ice time)

The Second Pairing—Your next-best defensemen. Perhaps home to that offensive whiz who isn't quite "first pairing" solid on the defensive front. Perhaps home to two depth defensemen who have better shut-down credentials than the top pairing. Regardless, like the big dogs, they see special teams time, too. (19-22 minutes of ice time)

The Third Pairing—Usually a pairing with some glaring deficiency, like size, skating ability, or a lack of experience. The fifth defenseman leads an exciting life, because he might have a new friend every other night, depending on the coach's decisions. Things you'll hear about them: "Well, of course they scored against the third pairing" or "Great effort, despite being the third pairing." (15-18 minutes of ice time)

Now, how do we arrive at the different combinations of players at forward and on defense?

Sometimes it'll come down to handedness. If a forward group has a dynamic right winger, it might look to pair a left-handed center with him because it's naturally easier for him to get that winger the puck.

Q: Why pull the goalie?

A: There are two reasons to pull your goalie. The first is when there's a delayed penalty, giving your team an extra attacker until the other team touches the puck to halt play.

The second is when a team is trailing late in the game and the goaltender heads to the bench for a sixth skater. This usually happens with less than two minutes remaining in a game, although we've seen aggressive (and somewhat maniacal) coaches like Patrick Roy pull his keeper with more than 13 minutes remaining in a game (and trailing by four goals, hence maniacal).

Does it work?

Andrew Thomas, in the *Journal of Quantitative Analysis*, found that 30 percent of the goals scored with one net empty were scored by the team with the empty net.

A research paper by David Beaudoin and Tim Swartz of Simon Fraser University on the 2007–08 season found that teams playing 6-on-5 score a goal every 8.5 minutes, which is far better than the 28.6 minutes for home teams and 26.2 minutes for road teams at 5-on-5. Another factor in favor of the extra attacker: the researchers found that 84 penalties were called on the team with the lead, versus 44 called on the team with the extra attacker, a nearly 1:2 ratio.

Ditto a right-handed center and a left winger, although it should be said that right-handed centers are rarer in the league. Of the top 60 centers in the 2013–14 season, only 21 were right-handed.

On defense, handedness is much more of a factor in creating pairings. Defensemen who play in an off-hand position—a right-handed defenseman playing left defense, for example—face a number of challenges in adjustment, from keeping the puck in the zone to effectively passing to their defensive partners.

Pull the goalie, get a power play, apparently.

War on Ice, the brilliant NHL stats site, ran 100,000 simulations to see whether the trailing team ties the game before the leading team scores another goal into an empty net. They found that the probability the trailing team ties the game is at its apex at 180 seconds remaining in the game when compared to the probability that the other team scores.

Or potentially lose the game if the opponent sends the puck into the gaping maw of your net.

A word about empty-net goals: they're not counterfeit, nor do the players see them that way.

First, because every goal next their names is a *goal,* whether it was into an empty net or deflected in or scored off their moneymaker. When it comes to contract talks, it doesn't matter how it was scored, just that it was scored.

Second, because scoring an empty-netter effectively ends the game, final-nail-in-the-coffin style. Which is why you'll see teams put out star players of questionable defensive prowess in the last two minutes—to find the open net and squeeze out the last breaths from an opponent.

(We're looking at you, Alex Ovechkin.)

For that reason, teams will specifically trade for a defenseman who is left-handed if they have a surplus of righties, and vice versa. One of the reasons the St. Louis Blues acquired Jay Bouwmeester in 2013, for example, was because he was a top-pairing lefty. They did it again after the following season in acquiring Carl Gunnarsson for Roman Polak. "As I say, to get a left-handed defenseman, you rob Peter to pay Paul. We have to give up a right-handed defenseman and a quality person," said Blues GM Doug Armstrong.

Robbing Peter! That's how important a left-handed defenseman is.

But most of the time, the combinations at forward and on defense have everything to do with time-tested chemistry. Some players' styles just mesh, whether it's a winger who can dig the puck to a sniping center or a small playmaking pivot whose hulking winger protects him; or, on defense, if a puck-moving defender is allowed to freelance thanks to his rock-solid pylon, er, "defensive defenseman," who is responsible in his own zone.

(Or if the average-to-mediocre center is friends off the ice with Phil Kessel. That too.)

Most coaches in the NHL design their forward groups by twos: pairing two players who have solid chemistry, usually a center and a winger, and then adding whatever type of player might best help them excel. For years, Sidney Crosby and Chris Kunitz had such chemistry, as the former's playmaking ability combined well with the latter's speed and ability to generate offense off the rush. To round out their line, the Pittsburgh Penguins would match them with a big-bodied grinder like Pascal Dupuis, who could create space for both of them.

And a trio like that will stay together through thick and thin. Unless, of course, they're coached by Michel Therrien, in which case their line will be broken up if they go scoreless on, like, two straight shifts.

GETTING BENCHED

NHL rules mandate that the players' bench must be 24 feet long and be able to accommodate 14 players, with protective glass tall enough to separate the animals from the zoo patrons. They also mandate that the doors to the players' bench must "swing inward" rather than out into the path of speeding players, and the fact this needs to be stated in the official rulebook is glorious validation of hockey's traditional disregard for knee ligaments.

Provided you're not watching a superhuman freak like Erik Karlsson or Alex Ovechkin, the average shift of an NHL skater is going to last between 45 and 50 seconds. A top-pairing NHL defenseman plays between 26 and 30 shifts per night, while a top-line NHL forward will have between 23 and 26 shifts per game, with the acknowledgement that some trend higher or lower.

All of this is to say that the bench area sees more action than a subway turnstile, only with slightly fewer weirdos.

Players have to be within five feet of the bench, and not engaged in the play when changing, before a teammate can hop on to replace him, or else they run the risk of earning a "too many men on the ice" penalty—provided the officials actually see it. (But of course *we* all do, when a TV analyst inevitably circles six or seven players on his monitor to shame the refs.)

Keep in mind that if a puck hits either player making a change accidentally, it's not a penalty. That's a very common misconception, especially for fans at the game screaming bloody murder over a rule they've never read.

Also important: the NHL rulebook actually states that a player has to change at the bench and use "no other exit." A darn shame for the home team, which should totally be allowed to use the Zamboni door to get off the ice during exhausting penalty kills. Let's make home-ice advantage an actual advantage beyond raucous fans and familiar bedding.

Head coaches typically manage the forwards. You'll see him tap a few players on the shoulders, getting them ready for their next shift, and then have another line on deck. When there's a chance for a change—if a team controls the puck or has it deep into the opposition's zone—there's a replacement for each player who leaves the ice. Center for center, wingers for wingers, each player immediately knowing his role for the next shift. Frequently, the players will call out each other's names so both know who is replacing whom.

Working in concert with the head coach is an assistant coach in charge of changing the defense. Sometimes, the defense pairings will be influenced by the forwards being sent out, e.g., having the top pairing playing with the top offensive line. And sometimes the pairings will be determined by whom the opponents put over the boards, as you always want your best shutdown defenseman to face the other team's top line, and have that D-man frequently paired with a team's best checking line.

Here's where things can get a little O.C.D. for coaches: line matching.

"I never liked playing for those coaches. Kind of annoying," recalled former NHL winger turned broadcaster Mike Johnson.

A coach will set up the next three lines after the one that's on the ice. But then, seeing what the other team puts out on the fly, he'll tell players at the very last second that it's their turn to hit the ice, even if they're not the next line in the rotation. That's because the opposing coach has done something—put out his top line, put out his bruising fourth line—to influence the line match.

For some coaches, this is the perfect system through which to defeat an opponent. For most observers, it's a handy way to unbalance your players' ice time to their detriment. Because in a league where the margins of victory are this slim, stapling the hindquarters of offensive players to the bench in lieu of overplaying a checking line is an express train to second-guessing.

WHAT TO WATCH WHEN YOU'RE WATCHING THE GAME

So that's what happens at the benches. But once the lines are deployed, there are a few things to keep an eye on as you watch the game, in the arena or on TV. We'll expand on some of these in later chapters, but for now:

Time on Ice

In general, the average shift length for an NHL player is around 45 seconds; it was 44.24 in the 2013–14 season. This stands in contrast with shift lengths even a decade ago, which were 7 percent longer, according to the blog Arctic Ice Hockey. Go back to the free-wheeling 1980s, and the shift length was upwards of 60 seconds. But fret not about the players' health—being that it was the 1980s, their bodies weren't taxed with playing any defense.

That's one of the keys for players: how much heavy lifting are they doing on each shift? The Detroit Red Wings would attempt to keep players like Henrik Zetterberg at around 40-second shifts in order to maintain their stamina for later in the game.

Keep an eye on which players have been out there the longest, but also what they've been doing: a defensive player running around in his own zone as an offense passes the puck around is going to be gassed at some point. If nothing else, you'll appreciate when a defensive player makes a Herculean effort to clear the puck before gliding over to the bench, winded.

As for those forwards who remain on the ice for too long, we'll pass the mic to venerable blogger Tyler Dellow:

"Being on the ice after a minute is sort of like being in a bar after 1:00 AM—there's no guarantee that something bad will happen, it's possible that something good will happen, but the odds are slanted heavily in favor of something bad."

The Star Chamber

Hockey isn't like basketball, where you see stars going head-to-head off the dribble. The CROSBY vs. OVECHKIN banner headlines on NHL.com are fun and all, but if you tallied up the time the two are actually on the ice together, it's roughly smaller than the Wicked Witch of the East's screen time before Dorothy dropped a house on her.

Instead, watch how teams decide to defend players like Ovechkin and Crosby. Which defensive pairings they throw out there on the reg. Which forwards are assigned to shadow them. And then watch the star player's line changes, and what sort of matchups his coach is trying to secure. How many shifts begin in the offensive zone? How many are in the defensive zone?

When Crosby faces the Montreal Canadiens, they make sure both center Tomas Plekanec and defenseman P.K. Subban are shadowing him. When Crosby plays the New York Rangers, they simply want to get defenseman Marc Staal to defend against him. And by "defend" we mean "vigorously cross-check him in the back of the head without any repercussions."

As we mentioned earlier, it's a chess match within the game for many coaches, and the star players are the kings among pawns.

Zone Starts

One of the great innovations in advanced stats is tracking zone starts, which tell us plenty about how a team uses a player, and the confidence that player has earned.

The offensive zone is where you'll glean the most.

Rookies, for example, are often protected with a large amount of starts in the attacking zone, mostly because the defensive side of the game has a hell of a learning curve in the NHL but also to maximize their offensive chances and bolster their confidence. In the 2014–15 season, David Pastrnak was an 18-year-old rookie sensation for the Boston Bruins, scoring 27 points in 46 games. The percentage of his shifts that began in the offensive zone: 47.4 percent, the highest for any player with at least 300 minutes played.

The same protection can be found for some defensemen who are either dynamic offensively or struggle a bit in their own end. Brian Campbell, a great offensive defenseman, started 40.7 percent of his shifts in the offensive zone and just 26 percent in the defensive zone in 2014–15; so often did his partner, rookie teenager Aaron Ekblad, thereby protecting him as well.

It works the other way, too. Forwards with the highest percentage of defensive zone starts are likely also ones with rather high faceoff-winning percentages, moderate to low ice time, and the scoring prowess to match. That's why it's always more impressive when a player posts an outstanding offensive season when starting most of his shifts in the D-zone—look no further than Phil Kessel in 2013–14, who tallied 54 points at 5-on-5 despite starting 37.3 percent of his shifts in the defensive zone. Which, of course, spoke to the Toronto Maple Leafs' ridiculous inability to get out of their own zone at times. Thanks, Randy Carlyle!

Breakouts and Entries

How a team gets out of its zone and how it enters the opposing zone are like bread slices around a BBQ sandwich: they're pretty much going to determine whether you've got something cohesive or tremendously sloppy (but potentially delicious).

When a team enters the attacking zone, it can chip-and-chase, dump-and-chase, or attempt to set up around the blue line. How much room an opposing defense surrenders at the line, and how smart the offensive team is with the puck, can make or break scoring chances.

When a team leaves its own zone, it's trying to organize in order to break down an opponent's forechecking system.

The Neutral Zone

This is where the game is won and lost. The seeds of a play are planted in how a team breaks out of its own zone. The neutral zone is where we find out if those seeds will grow into a mighty oak or be devoured by a hungry squirrel.

This is where the defensive team will set up in an effort to force a turnover, and where an attacking team will decide how to proceed into

Q. How do they keep stats at an NHL game?

A: With a tiny little pencil and a scorecard inside the game magazine, obviously...wait, no, that's baseball.

Official scoring at a hockey game is a multi-person task that involves a multitude of focuses. The jobs dramatically changed in the 1998–99 season, when "real-time scoring" was adopted by the league. Previously, shots that were blocked or missed weren't counted, among other stats. But that season, the league began having two stats entry scorers, two time-on-ice scorers (for home and away teams), and an event coordinator inside a room in the upper reaches of the arena, inputting data into computer programs that tabulate these numbers in real time.

These scorers can use video review to confirm on-ice events, but frequently rely on each other and "spotters" inside the room to attempt to accurately collect the information.

How accurate is it? As accurate as a human can get it. That's why many of the advanced stats we have in today's game that measure time on ice and puck possession are still only as good as the individuals collecting that data (more on how that might all radically change in the last chapter).

But if your question really is, "Does the home team get a little favoritism from the home team scorers?" then the answer is, "It depends on the category."

Most arenas are fairly accurate when it comes to shot attempts and time on ice. But a category like "hits" has become a punchline because (a) it's totally subjective and (b) some scorers have notoriously pumped up the hits totals for the home team's resident checker. But hey, it's not all bad: it puts food on Cal Clutterbuck's table.

the offensive zone. And that decision is going to dictate whether or not its time with the puck will result in a scoring chance being generated.

Analytics blogger Eric Tulsky found that there was a significant difference in offensive tactics from the neutral zone; the choice between dumping the puck in or attempting to carry it into the zone carry major repercussions.

"It appears that how a team gets the puck into the zone is as important as how often they do it," he wrote. "Maintaining possession of the puck at the blue line (carrying or passing the puck across the line) means a team will generate more than twice as much offense as playing dump and chase."

Yet watch how many times teams simply dump the puck over the defensemen and hope for the best while ceding possession back to the defense.

Faceoff Strategy

The faceoff doesn't just determine possession. It determines what the next two or three moves for a team will be after the draw. That's first going to be determined by the faceoff man—is he trying to draw it back to a shooter? Is he trying to tie up the puck in the dot to cause a little chaos? Did he actually lose the faceoff on purpose in order to keep the puck deep in the attacking zone? Because while it'll do nothing for his faceoff percentage, it's at times a reasonable tactic.

Obstruction

OK, tracking how players hook, hold, pick, and prevent creativity might sound about as exciting as watching paint dry during a public television pledge drive, but hear me out: seeing how players use these sneaky little moments to stymie an opponent or help each other out is the epitome of teamwork.

How a pick in the zone can spring a sniper for a scoring attempt, or how a little interference prevents an attacking player from getting into a scoring position. Is it a goal-sucking pox on the game that's ruining hockey for future generations? Sure! But it's also not going anywhere. Well, unless the referees decide to actually call obstruction on a consistent basis. But that would mean they're calling all of this on the level and aren't completely conspiring against your team.

Those Moments When the Puck Accidentally Hits the Referee during Play, and It Screws up Everything and You're Convinced He's Conspiring against Your Team

You know, those moments.

The Goalies

Are they active participants as "third defensemen," or do they remain in their crease when the puck is dumped in? Where are they directing rebounds? How often are they earning faceoffs? How active are they in policing their own crease? And, perhaps most of all: what's on their masks? Because in a league that preaches homogeny of uniforms and literally wants its players to be just one of a collection of numbers, the goalie mask is one of the lone bastions of individuality.

The Battle Zone

There are individual battles all over the ice during a game, but the one I focus on is always the one right in front of the crease.

The constant jostling for position between defensemen and forwards can be downright brutal; the jittery peek-a-boo movement of a goaltender as he tries to keep his eye on the shooter through two behemoths on his doorstep is a source of amusement. We might not have too many true garbage collectors in the NHL on the level of a Dave Andreychuk any longer, but we'll always have huge bodies doing their best to take the goalie's eyes away.

The less the goalie can see, the better the chance that someone's putting a puck behind him.

CHAPTER 2

FORWARDS AND SYSTEMS OVERLOAD

Picture the world of hockey like it's Hogwarts.

The general manager walks down a long, candlelit dining room aisle to your seat in front of the other young offensive wizards, carrying a weathered hat that smells of hockey gear and disappointment. He lowers it onto your head, and an animated mouth appears.

Where will you be sorted?

You have the flexibility of a senior citizen in skinny jeans, so you figure goaltending is out. You're a bit undersized and you shy away from the rough stuff, so you're pretty sure it won't be on defense. Your vision's perfect, so you won't be an on-ice official. Your heart isn't a cocktail of rage and depression with a megalomaniacal complex, so you certainly aren't a coach.

"Yes…yes…I see…" growls the hat.

You're left with three options. Seeing as you're of average height and weight and handle your faceoffs like a child learning to use chopsticks, playing center is out. You're a left-handed shot; maybe you'll be placed on your natural side on left wing to ward off defensemen along the boards as you carry through the zone; or, maybe the hat knows what kind of wicked sniper you fancy yourself as, and will place you on your off-wing on the right side.

"Yes…you're been sorted to…the house of SNIPER'IN," the hat rumbles.

Sweet. Right wing, pumping pucks from the circle like your name was Brett Hull. Endorsement deals! All-Star Game appearances! Long-term, high-cap-hit contracts the team will regret within a few years!

The world is yours, Sniper!

Ah, but what could have been at another forward spot.

GOING OFFENSIVE

The center is that person in your office who somehow knows how to fix the printer, unclog the toilet, change the coffee machine filters, and run the Super Bowl pool.

The center gets the play going off the faceoff but then transitions to a support role. In the offensive zone, that means positioning oneself to create a play when the winger has the puck. It depends on where the wings fly: if one winger has the puck and the other is set for a shot from the circle or the slot, the center goes to the net, either for a screen or a backdoor play on a pass. If one of those wingers is closer to the net, then the center will drop back to the high slot for a shot.

If also depends on what kind of center is on the ice. Someone like Joe Thornton of the San Jose Sharks is a playmaker, much more likely to hang at the half-boards (the straight section of the boards between the goal line and the blue line) and command the offense than aggressively crash the net. Sniping centers like Steven Stamkos and Jeff Carter are more likely to be found in a shooting lane.

No matter who the center is or what they're looking to accomplish, they all have the same responsibility: assisting the wingers in the offensive zone if they're outnumbered, and hauling ass back the other way as soon as the puck is turned over.

Q. What's a "suicide pass"?

A: It's mislabeled, that's what it is—it's a *homicide* pass.

It's a breakout pass from the defensive zone to a forward streaking into the neutral zone that generally puts him on the "trolley tracks," aka in the path of an onrushing defensive player who lays him out. It's also usually a pass that has him glancing down at his skates or struggling to corral the puck with his stick.

When you see a huge open-ice hit on an unsuspecting player, there are many factors involved that made him unsuspecting. But more often than not, it's because a teammate uncorked a pass that served up his head on a platter for a defender.

Like we said, the center has more jobs than a kid saving for college.

But the wingers? A list of their responsibilities in the offensive zone breaks down as follows:

1. Hit people in the corners.
2. Score.
3. Failing to accomplish No. 2, find someone else who can.

In theory, all three forwards are working in concert to create offensive chances, which is what you see in a well-executed cycle.

CYCLE LIKE THE SEDINS

Larry Robinson is a Hall of Fame defenseman and a Stanley Cup–winning coach. Back in his playing days in the 1970s and 1980s, preventing three forwards from cycling in the offensive zone was easy: just clutch, grab, interfere, and generally pummel them with little to no recourse.

But you can't do that in today's NHL, which is why the offensive zone is fertile ground for the cycle to work its magic.

"What you're trying to do is keep possession of the puck, because that is key in the offensive zone, but you're also trying to get the other team to start running around," Robinson told NHL.com in 2011. "You can almost create a pick situation because the defense is running around so much. It's like a set play in basketball where you're trying to create an open shot."

If you love the team aspect of hockey, then the cycle is your catnip. It requires synchronization, timing, physicality, and above all else an understanding of teammates' tendencies.

It also helps if you're identical twins, as Henrik and Daniel Sedin turned the cycle into something symphonic, to the point where "Cycle Like the Sedins" is praise of the highest order.

Here's how it works: picture a triangle, with two corners facing the boards. One forward (F1) has the puck toward the left corner. Another forward (F2) is trailing him at the right corners. The top corner of the triangle finds that third forward (F3) in the high slot. The F1 moves the puck back to the F2 along the boards, and the F2 then becomes the left corner of the triangle. The F3 skates over to the right corner, where the F2 was previously. The F1, who originally had the puck? That forward moves back to the top corner in the high slot, with three options: preparing for a shot, preparing to get back on defense in the event of a turnover, or preparing to hop back into the cycle should it continue.

Again, it's about tendencies. At some point, two cyclers might hook up for a set play, with one breaking the cycle to go to the net on a feed from the other. Or the wheel just churns in the corner for a bit, getting closer and closer to the goal line, trying to get the defense tuckered out and out of position.

You know what else tuckers out defenders? Two hundred pounds of human blunt force crashing into them in the corners.

CYCLING

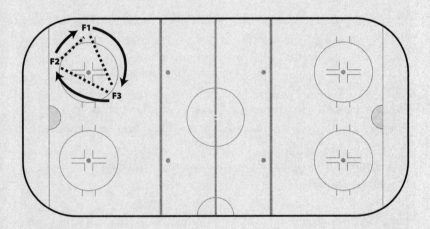

HUMAN WRECKING BALLS

One of my favorite line pairings in hockey history is the Crash Line: center Bobby Holik with wingers Mike Peluso and Randy McKay.

They were the checking line for the 1995 Stanley Cup champion New Jersey Devils, but in name only: the "crash" was a reference to their ferocious forechecking, which created more offensive chances than some of the more traditional goal-scoring lines did. If advanced stats existed in the mid-1990s, one assumes they'd be puck-possession leaders. Also, hockey arguments would have been exponentially more nuanced and annoying in the mid-1990s.

That line was the first to make me appreciate the human-wrecking-ball aesthetic of forechecking. An offensive player chips the puck in; it then becomes a combination of chess match and blunt force trauma. Ideally, you never want to dump the puck in and have to chase it. You want to keep possession. But here's the thing: NHL defensemen are *really, really* good. So, sometimes you just have to dump and chase, even if it means giving up possession of the puck.

The first man in on the forecheck is called the F1, followed by the F2 and F3.

"The first guy in should force them to angle it up the wall. We were very aggressive, pinching in our defense," said former Nashville Predators assistant Brent Peterson. "Some teams don't pinch in their defense at all. It's all based on what a coach thinks his team is best at.

"The bottom line is that in this league, you have to be right on the defensemen's asses."

Here are a few different forechecking options that teams can deploy.

The 2-1-2 Forecheck

This is the most common forechecking system. Two players go after the puck on a dump into the corner, either strong wide or weak side. The F1 is tasked with trying to acquire the puck; the F2 is his backup plan, skating in to pressure behind him; the F3 goes to the slot to either take a pass for a shot, assist in the opposite corner if the puck is moved ahead, or to get back on defense if the forecheck fails.

The benefit of the 2-1-2 is that it takes away a lot of ice from a team trying to break out of its own zone. The drawback is that due to its commitment of two players deep and other moving pieces, there are times when a pinching defenseman could get caught low and the high forward in the zone could end up playing the role of defenseman. And that can be downright ugly on a breakout the other way.

The 1-2-2 Forecheck

The Boston Bruins used this system under coach Claude Julien, which helps when you have a dynamic two-way center like Patrice Bergeron.

2-1-2 FORECHECK

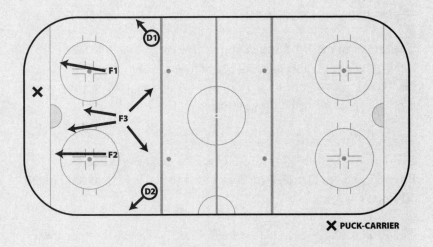

X PUCK-CARRIER

1-2-2 FORECHECK

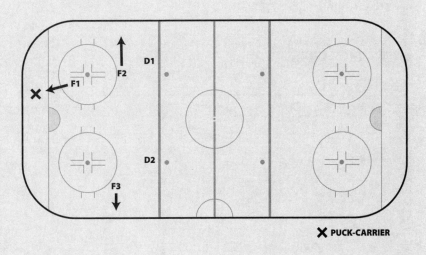

X PUCK-CARRIER

The F1 flies in solo to attack the defenseman; to either hit him to take the puck away or angle in to force a pass. The system gives the boards as an option to the defense, but then the F2 and F3 quickly take it away.

The benefit of the 1-2-2 is that you've only committed one man deep if the other team is able to break out of its own zone. The drawback is that by committing one forechecker, you're giving a team slightly more time and space to escape your pressure.

The 2-3 Forecheck

Ever hear of the Left Wing Lock? That's the defensive system Scotty Bowman and the Detroit Red Wings used to perfection, and this is an offshoot.

The F1 and F2 aggressively forecheck. The F3—usually but not always the left wing—hangs back and acts as a third defenseman, playing the middle of the ice between the two D-men. If the forecheckers get the puck, the F3 moves in on the attack. If they don't…well, you're in pretty good shape with a top defensive forward and two defensemen back to guard the rush.

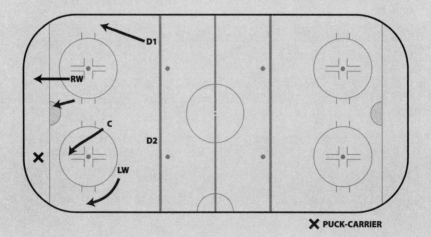

LEFT WING LOCK

✕ PUCK-CARRIER

The benefit: you *really* have your backside covered. The drawback: not the most vigorous offensive system, and something you see teams slip into when protecting a lead.

Speaking of a lack of offense. Well, at least that's the misconception....

THE EVIL GLORY OF THE TRAP

The systems described here are ones implemented in the attacking zone on the forecheck. But the same types of formations are used in the neutral zone when the other team possesses the puck—attempting to clog the middle of the ice to slow the attack or, more to the point, reacquire the puck and transition to offense.

"Clog the middle!" Ugh, the phrase itself is off-putting, conjuring images of gunk-covered hairballs causing your drain to overflow. To that end, think of the neutral zone trap as the clog that requires two bottles of drain flush and the big twisty metal snake.

The first thing that needs to be established about the neutral zone trap is that it predates the 1995 New Jersey Devils, the Stanley Cup champions who shockingly swept the supremely talented Detroit Red Wings by trapping them into frustrating oblivion.

Perhaps the most famous example was the Montreal Canadiens of the 1970s, who would deploy the trap when necessary but not with the frequency we saw it have in the 1990s. (A team whose coach, Scotty Bowman, imported that style from Europe. The same Scotty Bowman who would praise the trap even as it suffocated his Red Wings in 1995. Stand-up guy, that one.)

The scheme was an odd mix of passive and aggressive play. It could be correctly labeled as a 1-4 defensive scheme, with one forward pressuring the puck-carrier, forcing him to one side or another. The rest of the defense hangs back closer to the defensive zone, but as soon as there's an inkling of trouble for the offensive player, those defenders collapse

THE TRAP

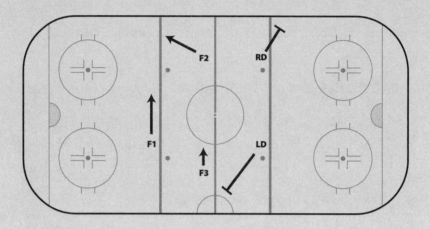

around him—a "trap" in the "neutral zone," if you will. (Hockey is nothing if not creative with its nicknames.)

Now, here's the dirty little secret about the neutral zone trap: the best defense is a good offense.

Why is the defending team trying to steal the puck? To add it to the collectibles it keeps in its rec room? Hell no: it's attempting to steal the puck so it can transition and put the puck in the opposing net.

The 1995 Devils, scourge of the NHL? They were tied for 13th in team scoring during that truncated lockout season. In Jacques Lemaire's first season at the helm, in 1993–94? The Devils scored 306 goals as a team, good for second in the NHL, right behind…the Red Wings' 356 goals, aka the team they would stymie for the Stanley Cup the following season.

"I'm real sick of hearing all the criticism. It's ridiculous, when we hold a team to 17 shots and we get 28 and a lot of quality scoring chances," said Devils defenseman Ken Daneyko.

Which brings us to a salient debate: is the neutral zone trap really all that bad?

The 1990s were an expansion boom for the NHL, which was great news for league revenue but less so for quality of play. The Mighty Ducks of Anaheim and the Florida Panthers both used the trap around the same time Jacques Lemaire brought it to New Jersey.

You have to remember that in the early 1990s, the NHL was still on a contact high from the go-go-Gretzky 1980s scoring boom. In 1990–91, there were seven teams that scored 290 goals or more on the season. But in 1993–94, that number was down to five, and by 1996–97 that number was down to zero. Ditto 1997–98, when no teams broke 290 goals but five of them couldn't crack 200 goals. Back in 1991, there wasn't a team that scored fewer than 220 on the season.

The NHL's brain trust, and many of its general managers, were concerned about these diminishing offensive returns, and point to the rise of the trap as the reason. The 1994 GM meetings discussed the trap and how to prevent it. Bobby Clarke—the ferocious defensively oriented forward who starred on the Philadelphia Flyers in the 1970s— was the general manager of the Florida Panthers and pummeled the anti-trap crowd like they were the Soviets.

As Clarke told the *Baltimore Sun*, "Some of the guys who are doing the squawking didn't win playing wide-open. Now they're not winning with close checking. It's easier to blame the other team's style than to look in the mirror. Everyone [complains] about the high scoring in the All-Star Game. They don't like that. They don't like what we do. All they want is their own team to win.

"Ah, let them change the rules. We'll play any way they want to play. We forecheck. We don't sit back and wait. We go after it. We'll compete. We'll play. The teams doing the crying are just jealous. They're a bunch of babies. We're not supposed to have babies in the NHL, but we've got 'em. They cry about our style of play. They cry about officials. They cry and cry. They always find an excuse for losing. They're just crybabies."

The "crybabies" would eventually get their way, just over a decade later.

Legislation against the trap was incremental and, frankly, that was to the league's detriment. The have-not teams that used the trap played a different kind of defense than, say, the Devils. Consider that New Jersey had legendary goalie Martin Brodeur, Hall of Fame defensemen Scott Stevens and Scott Niedermayer, and a collection of other NHL talent that could be top-line players anywhere else in the league. Now, consider what many expansion teams and pale imitations of the Devils were rolling out there: none of that.

They'd ice teams with third-liners playing top-line minutes, with second defensive pairings that wouldn't be able to crack the lineup on the league's elite teams. The Devils and other talented teams would play "positional defense"—the trap, for sure, but one that relied on speed and defensive opportunism to generate turnovers and their own offensive chances. The expansion teams, and others that didn't have elite teams' depth, would play a style that was built on rampant interference and obstruction.

"In my mind, the trap is a fancy word for interference," GM David Poile once said.

Others spoke up about it, most notably Mario Lemieux of the Pittsburgh Penguins. He once infamously called the NHL a "garage league" when penalties weren't being whistled; he would consistently bemoan the amount of interference that crept into the game.

But even ardent critics were joining the ranks of the trappers. Like in 1998, when New York Rangers coach Colin Campbell—who once demonized the Devils as an "interchangeable flock of forwards"— adopted the system.

"It's a bad word, I know. But we're going to the trap. Right now, we can't score and we can't protect a lead. Everyone is winning with it. We want to frustrate teams the way they frustrate us. We have to keep trying new things," he said.

To restate the question we're noodling through: is the neutral zone trap really all that bad?

The system itself isn't. When played well by teams with the proper levels of talent, it's actually an effective way to generate offense. Perhaps the last great example was Guy Boucher's Tampa Bay Lightning.

A mercurial, confident coach, Boucher implemented a 1-3-1 trap system with the Lightning. In his first year (2010–11), the Bolts were seventh in the league in goals scored. In his second year, they were ninth. And yet the passive scheme he had his team play frustrated

Q. Is it ever not the puck-carrier's fault if a play goes offside?

A: Let's begin by establishing the rule.

IT'S OFFSIDE, NOT "OFFSIDES."

OK, that established, offside is when a player on the attacking team precedes the puck into the offensive zone, with both skates completely across the blue line before the puck is. This doesn't apply to the puck-carrier, as long as he has possession of the puck. Also, an attacking zone player can literally be standing an inch from the goalie with the puck outside the zone, but would be onside if a defending player carries or passes the puck into his own end.

Now, is it always the puck-carrier's fault when he goes offside?

If offensive hockey is about timing, the puck-carrier keeps the beat. So when you see a team go offside, it's like the drummer decided to do a fancy-pants solo in the middle of the song only to drop his sticks. The band stops playing, starts glaring, and there are stern words before the encore.

So yes, it's almost completely the puck-carrier's fault. Unless of course the defenseman made a play, in which case it's still the puck-carrier's fault for being so sloppy with the puck to allow this calamity to happen.

BREAKING THE TRAP 1

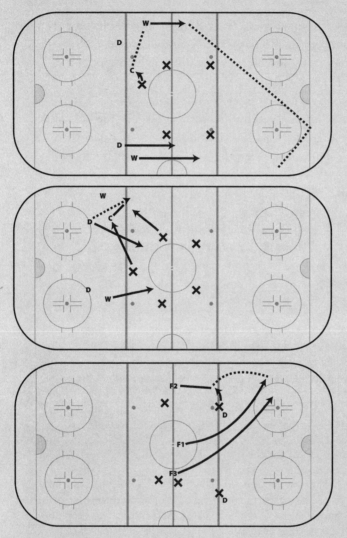

Here are three strategies an offense might employ to beat the trap:

Top: The center carries the puck and passes it to the left wing, who gains the red line and then sends the puck to the far corner of the offensive zone, hoping the right wing will reach it first and control.

Middle: The center carries the puck through the middle of the ice until he meets the defense, then drops it for his defenseman, who moves through the vacated space with a breaking right wing.

Bottom: The puck-carrier attempts to chip the puck behind the defense, sending it off the boards and into the corner as the other two forwards crash to control.

opponents so much, the Philadelphia Flyers actually just held the puck and stopped skating in a 2011 game, which the *Wall Street Journal* called "the worst hockey game ever."

But again: the Lightning that season had Steven Stamkos, Martin St. Louis, and Vinny Lecavalier to help turn the system's turnovers into goals.

Other teams that used the trap in the last two decades weren't blessed with that talent. Their style of defense was unwatchable but effective in keeping games close and those teams close to contention. This being a copycat league, others adopted it. Soon, the NHL's brand of hockey was characterized by soccer scores and offensive stars who weren't coming close to the stats posted during the early 1990s.

In 2003–04, 11 teams scored fewer than 200 goals during the season, and that was that. During the lockout that killed the 2004–05 season, the NHL put together a rules and regulations camp headed by Red Wings star Brendan Shanahan that sought to create ways to eliminate the trap as a game-long tactic.

Their solution: ratchet up the enforcement of obstruction rules; "taking out the red line" to allow long stretch passes through the neutral zone defense; and, most importantly, creating the "goalie trapezoid" that restricted where a netminder could play the puck, cutting into their role as a "third defenseman."

As a game-long, season-long tactic, the trap was finally broken.

But it's never going away. Even today, you see elite teams hunker down and "clog the neutral zone" when they have a lead. Even today, you see accusations and much consternation about "boring trap hockey" creeping back into the league.

That's because defense wins championships, and because everyone on the ice has been forced to up their game defensively—especially at the forward spot.

GOING BOTH WAYS

Chris Chelios is a Hall of Fame defenseman who once said of his chosen position: "It takes brains. It's not like a forward, where you can get away with scoring and not play defense."

Le ouch.

» ODD MEN AND THEIR RUSHES

Oh! How exciting! Your team has a 2-on-1 break the other way! Now how will they screw it up....

The 2-on-1 odd-man rush is, to me, the single most exhilarating offensive play in hockey, now that the shootout has watered down the spontaneity of the breakaway. It might also be one of the most frustrating, because HOW CAN YOU NOT SCORE WITH TWO FORWARDS AGAINST ONE DEFENSEMAN?

The basic building block for odd-man rush success? Confusion. Making the goalie and the defender have to guess shot, pass, or a move that will lead to a higher-percentage shot. The puck-carrier is the one who's going to determine how to play it, based on what the defenseman chooses to take away. The other forward is either a triggerman or a decoy, but in either case he needs to be ready for a one-timer if a pass gets through.

A 3-on-2 odd-man rush adds a few more decisions. The F1 (the puck-carrier) will typically swing wide to one wing while another offensive player (F3) swings wide to the other. The third man in (F2) trails them slightly. Now, the F1 has a multitude of options: get selfish and take the shot, hoping for a rebound; pass it back to F2; or pass it toward the crease in the hopes that F3 deflects it.

Another variation: the F2 goes to the net like a rocket, and the F3 slides over to the high slot. So now you've likely attracted a defenseman to cover the player rushing to the net, which could leave that F3 wide open for a chance.

Of course, none of this will ultimately work, and your team will squander an odd-man chance...and then score on some fluky shot from center ice minutes later. Because hockey is why.

That's entirely unfair, mind you. Centers are essential in stopping opposing scoring chances, and not just because they're the first line of defense in the faceoff circle. (Hence, 28 of the first 37 winners of the Selke Trophy for best defensive forward were centers.)

And while wingers still get labeled as goal-hangers or cherry-pickers or, worse yet, Russian, the bottom line is that in today's NHL there's no room for wingers who can't effectively back-check or position themselves in the defensive zone to transition to offense. Because it's, like, the easiest job on the ice.

Every forward essentially has the same aim in the defensive zone—do not allow the puck to enter the net, ensure that the puck is cleared over the blue line. For wingers, that means supporting the center and defensemen who are doing the heavy lifting, and getting ready to transition to offense.

Look at the offensive zone. Picture a triangle that extends from the half-boards to the blue line, then down to the slot and then back to the half-boards. This is the winger's defensive domain, attempting to disrupt both the defenseman's shot and his passing opportunities deeper in the zone. In other words, limiting his opponent's options.

The winger on the "weak side" stays between the hash-marks and the top of the circle, keeping his stick pointed toward the blue line. This allows him to collapse in the zone to the crease if his team needs defensive support.

The winger on the "strong side" is going to challenge the opposing defensemen a little more, watching out for both the defenseman trying to skate around him and a pick play from an opposing forward to spring that aforementioned defenseman.

(And those buggers are *fast* in the NHL. Tyler Johnson of the Tampa Bay Lightning told me once that his first "welcome to the show" moment was attempting to defend Kris Letang of the Penguins at the

» THREE ESSENTIAL TRUTHS ABOUT FACEOFFS

1. Losing a draw isn't always bad.
While the name of the game is always going to be "possess the puck at all costs," sometimes the means to that end is allowing the opponent the upper hand on a faceoff.

Ryan Getzlaf of the Anaheim Ducks, for example, will intentionally lose draws in the offensive zone if he feels his line has a significant speed advantage over its opponents. Hence, the opposing center would get the puck in deep, and one of Getzlaf's wingers would win a race to the corner for possession.

"The [faceoff-winning-percentage] stat is a little bit skewed in the fact that it's not always about who won the draw," Getzlaf told the *OC Register*. "It's more about who comes out with it. Because in the offensive zone, you do different things. You try different things."

Another thing a center might try: losing a faceoff early in the game to get an opponent looking for a certain tendency. Because, in the end...

2. It's all a big mind game.
After a while, centers know each other's tendencies. So the key to being successful in the faceoff circle is to outguess your opponent and keep them guessing.

blue line and then getting deked out of his skates. Happens to the best of them.)

But the best defense is a good offense, and that's why effective breakouts are essential. Watch what a winger does near the boards when his defensemen or his center get a turnover. If he comes off the wall, it gives him several offensive options, from clearing the puck off the glass to finding a streaking teammate leaving the zone. If an opposing player is coming in, the primary reaction from a winger should be to turn his back on the play and protect the puck at all costs...with the full

Patrice Bergeron may go down as one of the best faceoff men in NHL history. His prowess in the circle is predicated on many things—speed, physicality—but also on adaptability.

"He's not very predictable," said NBC broadcaster Eddie Olczyk. "Sometimes he'll knife in there and get it, sometimes he'll hit and pull, sometimes he'll just go for a tie-up and get some help. It keeps the guy on the other side on his toes. He can really win it any way—forehand, backhand, with his feet. There aren't many guys who can do that."

3. Everyone's a cheater.

Cheating at the dot isn't just rampant, it's expected. Every postseason, there are accusations about one team or another cheating on draws because someone's trying to gain an advantage from the linesmen.

But cheating goes beyond winning or losing a draw; it's also a tactic through which a team can get a little breather after, say, being forced to remain on the ice after icing the puck. Coaches might send a winger in to take a draw who has no intention of doing anything but getting tossed out of the circle by a linesman; in comes the center (aka the person they actually want to take the faceoff) and the team adds a few more hearts to its health meter in the meantime.

The NHL has actively tried to remedy this by having the initial faceoff guy move back from 12 to 18 inches rather than being tossed, with a second violation earning a delay-of-game penalty. But it doesn't change the fact that teams will still use faceoffs as a chance to catch their collective breath.

acknowledgement that a hit into his back from an opposing player will likely earn a power play.

Hey, if the referees are to call it, might as well draw it.

Centers in the defensive zone are typically referred to as "third defensemen," which I guess means puck-handling goalies are actually "fourth defensemen," and you start to understand why it's so damn hard to score in this game.

In theory, the center and the defensemen go up against the three attacking forwards. The defensemen hang low near the goal—one working the puck-carrier, one planted in front of the crease like a bishop guarding a king—while the center takes care of the space between them and the high slot. The center's job is to limit offensive options for opposing players, which means trying to keep passing lanes more clogged than Jabba the Hutt's arteries.

If the action moves behind the goal line, the center is usually tasked with policing the slot, making sure he doesn't get caught below the net. Because if he does, it probably means there's an offensive player in the slot with his stick raised for a shot, like those fat dudes in Nintendo *Ice Hockey* ready to rocket one on the goalie.

Basically, centers need to have a split personality: the ability to lead the rush and the ability to pivot back to defense. It's one of the reasons why young centers get chewed up and spit out defensively in the NHL, because the defensive side of the job is a dramatic change from their days in college and junior hockey.

In fact, most young players begin as centers. Before the Sorting Hat decides their goal-scoring is too potent to worry about such responsibilities, and places them in CELLYTHERYN.

"Expecto Puckronum!"

CHAPTER 3

THE ART OF GOAL-SCORING

Wayne Gretzky is famous for an incalculable number of things, and one of them is a quote that the late Apple CEO Steve Jobs converted into a mantra:

"Help, I'm a terrible coach and the Coyotes stink and the NHL owes me, like, $9 million...."

No, wait, that's not it....

"I skate to where the puck is going to be, not where it has been."

It's the perfect summary of what made Gretzky the top goal-scorer in the history of hockey (since Mario Lemieux lost all that time to ailments and Jaromir Jagr lost all that time to work stoppages and the KHL and both had to play in an era that featured actual defense).

Gretzky's anticipation of a play developing is the essential ingredient for goal-scoring, and especially in the NHL. It's just that he was able to do it better than anyone else the game has ever seen.

"If you take a high-school gym class, and everyone's facing the tennis ball, moving as a pack, the person who gets out of that pack and goes to the open area and waits for the ball, that person is going to score," said Justin Bourne, a former ECHL player turned hockey columnist. "You need time and space to shoot the puck."

Q. Who has the advantage in shootouts: goalies or shooters?

A: The penalty shot was one of the most exciting plays in hockey until the shootout turned it into a weekly occurrence. Stripped of its uniqueness, this visceral thrill has been transformed into pedestrian tedium.

But we digress....

Statistically, goalies have the advantage when it comes to penalty shots: from 2005 to 2014, there wasn't a single season in which the penalty shot success rate for shooters was over 40 percent. With an increased sample size in the shootout, that percentage drops even lower: from 2005 to 2014, the average scoring rate in the shootout was just 32.97 percent.

In the 2013–14 season, goalies had a collective .684 save percentage. Shooters scored 413 goals on 1,305 shots against.

So it's still a goalie's gimmick to lose.

A typical hockey shot takes about a second to execute. In that second, and before the defense pins you down, there's not much time for aiming or picking holes on a goaltender.

When you're a good goal-scorer, you don't think about trying to score when you're shooting the puck. Sure, you have an idea where you want it to go, and what might happen next based on the velocity, but you just trust your body and take the shot because you feel that's where it *should* go. And the great ones are better at getting it there than most.

Every NHL player grows up emulating players like Gretzky. Many follow the same template he did to score goals. But without that intangible blessing of talent from the Hockey Gods, few can ever be mentioned in the same book volume, let alone sentence.

GETTING YOUR SHOT

In the NBA, entire plays are schemed out in order to give top scorers "their shot." The shot they've taken since they could first dribble. The shot they practice for hours in the gym. Give them the rock in that spot, and they'll sink it.

The same holds true in the NHL…except there's a guy with inflated pads and a catching glove standing in front of the goal. (Seriously, every NBA game would be 10–8 if they had goalies, and every NHL game would be 10–8 if they had a shot clock.)

Recall a player like the recently retired Martin St. Louis, one of the most consistently lethal goal-scorers in the last 15 years. He's a left-handed shot. He had one spot on the ice where he liked to set up shop for "his shot": a knee-to-the-ice, falling-down snipe from the lower edge of the right circle.

Watch a player like Alex Ovechkin, who might end his career as one of the top five goal-scorers in NHL history. He's a right-handed shot. His shot is a one-timer from the left circle. He goes there at 5-on-5. He plants himself there on the power play (after some years when he was foolheartedly placed at the point). Everyone knows the shot is coming, and yet goalies have to watch out for whiplash as it flies past them.

Watch a player like Wayne Simmonds. He's a right-handed shot who also happens to be 6-foot-2. Over time, he found his sweet spot, too: in front of the crease, giving his teams one of the best "net-front presence" players in the NHL; a player who can screen with the best of them, but also collect the garbage (i.e., loose pucks and rebounds) like his forbearers Dave Andreychuk and Tomas Holmstrom would.

All of these wingers set up shop in their respective kitchens not just because that's where the majority of their goals are scored, but because *their linemates* know that's where the majority of their goals are scored.

Think about an NFL quarterback dropping back in the pocket. Some receivers run downfield. A running back sprints to the QB's left, a safety valve in case other options are taken away.

Same thing with an offensive star setting up in his spot. The puck-handler gets in trouble, but he knows he'll have someone waiting at a particular spot on the ice. It's about tendencies. Watching how they develop in the flow of even-strength play is one of the benefits of watching the game live. (Of course, there are always scorers who are more in the tradition of Ovechkin and Stamkos, who could get their shots away skating in slush with one glove behind their backs.)

The sniper can also rely on his teammates to create room for him through the glorious tradition of illegal picks.

OK, make that "quasi-legal picks, but pretty much illegal." It's one of those plays, like diving, that can be easily shrouded by an offensive player under the cloak of legality. You see, it can be like Grand Central Station in the offensive zone, what with the 10 skaters and the goalie and the on-ice officials. Sometimes players just bounce off each other, like atoms in an electromagnetic field. The key for an offensive player is to bounce off a defender as if it's in the natural flow of play—say, after making a pass to a trailing teammate and then *Whoops look at that I've accidentally skated right into you as I glide through the attacking zone sorry!*

The beautiful thing about a pick play is that more often than not the offensive player can mask it successfully, putting the onus on the defender to get around the pick. Which means it's either make contact with an offensive player and get taken out of the play, or attempt to avoid that player and still get taken out of the lane, opening it up for a shooter.

A smart puck-carrier is going to lead defensive players right into his teammates in the offensive zone, like fighter jets in a dogfight trying to lure a bogey into the shooting range of a wingman. This frequently happens down in the corners, as the puck-carrier is being hounded by a defender and has a teammate trailing him in the cycle. If he cuts back

ALL-TIME GOALS CREATED

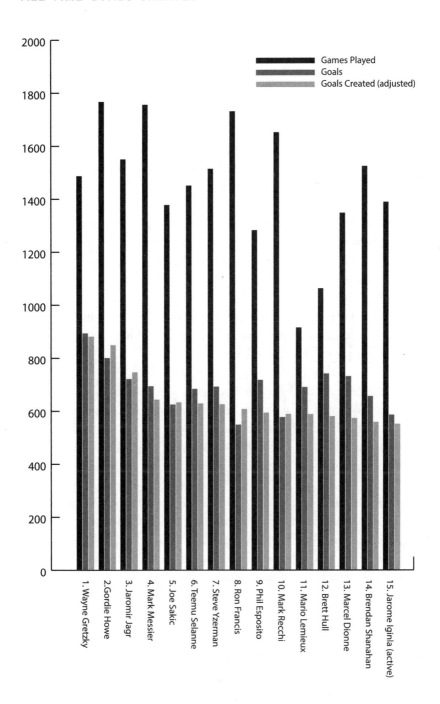

quickly, chances are the defender is going to skate right into that trailing player, springing the puck-holder for a scoring chance. Because what else was that teammate supposed to do—*avoid him?*

The thing about the pick play: subtlety works but obvious is usually going to draw a call. In that way it's like the NFL: a pick play on a 10-yard pass from quarterback to receiver might not earn a flag, but it's darn sure going to get one when it's a pick in the end zone. Same thing in the NHL: a pick play during 5-on-5 might be masked and ignored, but a pick play on the power play, for example—the shooter in the high slot who *just so happens* to bump into a penalty-killer as he cuts across the zone—is going to be too obvious not to earn a call.

The power play is a different animal for shooters. At even strength, it's less about set plays and more about tendencies. On the power play, it can look like an NBA offensive set: cycling the puck around the zone to get a star player his shot.

Ovechkin is one of the most lethal power-play shooters the NHL has ever seen, and one of the reasons is that the Washington Capitals would run their power play through him.

He'll stand near the left circle like a gunslinger—stick in his hands, slowly gliding to his shooting lane. Some teams will pressure him without the puck, which is begging the Capitals to take further advantage of the off-man opportunity. Most will lay off Ovechkin and allow him his shot.

When the puck comes to him, it's on full blast, every time: his stick raised high in the air, his right knee dropped to the ice, his shot like a clothesline strung between his stick and the netminder. If the goalie is lucky enough to stop it, the puck's velocity could immediately lead to another chance, but often, he's not so lucky.

It sometimes appears the Capitals power play exists to get that shot for Ovechkin, as other power plays cater to snipers on other teams. What makes these setups so lethal is that they create an expectation that can be subverted for an even more effective offensive chance—Ovechkin will, at times, forego his one-timer for a sprint to the crease, setting up hockey's version of an alley-oop on the power play.

Although comparing the distance on his shots to Ovechkin's is like comparing a marathon to collecting your newspaper at the foot of the driveway, Wayne Simmonds is also a player who looks for "his shot" on the power play, and his team filters the puck to him.

Simmonds is one of the NHL's best "net-front players," although that label is a bit deceptive. He frequently stands to the side of the net, providing a target for passes across the crease. But he's also blessed with the wingspan of a pterodactyl, which allows him to deflect pucks on goal from that wide angle.

"I've got really long arms, so if someone's boxing me out, sometimes I can still get that extra inch or two inches, just enough to get my stick on the puck. People may see I'm not the heaviest or the biggest guy, but I think I use that to my advantage," Simmonds told ESPN.com in 2014.

His positioning and athleticism allow his teammates the option of passing down to him for a chance at the side of the net, or to wait for him to provide a proper screen in front of the netminder. His lanky frame won't exactly block out the goalie's vision, but his quickness allows him to move around the crease and collect rebounds.

The power play is as methodical as even strength is designed to be chaotic.

But sometimes you need a little chaos on the power play, a little unpredictability. Like, for example, when a shot looks like it's headed straight for the goalie's padding, and then suddenly changes course on the way to net, floating by him.

Q: What's the greatest virtue of a goal-scorer?

A: An excellent, not-all-that-easy question to answer. Pretty much could be a second volume of this book on its own.

Every goal-scorer who dots the top 50 in NHL history has his own virtues. Wayne Gretzky had the greatest hockey sense in history. Mario Lemieux had the size and the hands, Gordie Howe had the size and the hands and the nasty streak. Pavel Bure and Mike Gartner had the speed and the release. Jaromir Jagr was a comet for most of his career and then became an immovable object in the offensive zone, backing into defenders like Tim Duncan looking for a foul.

If you ask those in the game, you hear a lot about three aspects:

1. **Timing:** The ability to fire a puck fast and accurately when given the opportunity, and the ability to keep the puck until the time is right. It's that sweet spot between possession and possessing too long that goal-scorers seem to find.

2. **Going to the net:** The fearless ability to go to the "dirty part" of the ice and score goals.

What was once predictable becomes unpredictable. And while deflections are successful due to a not-insignificant amount of luck, they're also as much a skill as a slapper or a wrister are for a shooter.

THE ART OF DEFLECTION

Full disclosure: when I first started watching hockey, I figured all the players scoring on puck deflections had absolutely no flippin' clue what they were doing.

3. Hockey sense: The nebulous, un-quantifiable thing that separates Marian Hossa from Marcel Hossa. Well, amongst other things.

So what's the greatest virtue? Honestly, some of it depends on the era. Having blazing speed isn't going to serve you well if teams are allowed to obstruct and clog up the ice. Having great hands but bad wheels is only going to get you so far if the league's rules make every night a track meet.

But there is a through-line that connects the generations of goal-scorers, from the actual Maurice "Rocket" Richard to the guys who win the Maurice "Rocket" Richard Trophy today:

Processing speed.

The elite goal-scorers are on fiber optic while the rest of the league is using dial-up. They can understand time, space, quality of competition, quality of goaltender, and the type of move necessary to score, and do all of this in the time it takes for you to raise your backside from your arena seat.

As Paul Maurice said of Ron Francis, he of the 549 career goals: "He'd go to a spot you didn't think he should be and then, the puck was there! That's fine once. But he'd do it over and over again."

You just can't teach that.

The puck is so small! The stick blades are so thin! What sort of sorcery was this?

I remember the first time I mentioned this sentiment to a player, and it was a bit like seeing Yo-Yo Ma's reaction after telling him a trained monkey could match his cello virtuosity. Years of practice, moments of precision timing, all of it tossed to the side by a rank amateur who confused practiced skill with perceived luck.

The fact is that a deflection goal has more valor than any other type of goal scored, because your "shot" only happens after another player fires the puck in your direction. You have to risk your wellbeing in order to get the high reward of a difficult save for the goalie behind you.

"There's a certain element of bravery to go into that area, with pucks coming in high and defensemen tying up your stick and pushing you out of there," said Hall of Fame center Joe Nieuwendyk, to *The New York Times* in 2012. "For people who want to score goals and get their noses dirty, that's where you have to be."

Nieuwendyk is a great example of the changing face of puck deflection. First, like John Tavares and many other players, he had a background in lacrosse, and that skillset translated well when it came to deflecting pucks.

During his heyday with the Calgary Flames, Nieuwendyk had all the time and space he needed to knock home the puck because his team's top defenseman, Hall of Famer Al MacInnis, had one of the most powerful shots in the history of the league.

But that was before every defensive player was geared up in protective layers. Today's shots from the point have to pass through defenders who will freely sacrifice their bodies to block the puck, adding a challenge for the puck-deflectors, who have to pick up the puck off their teammate's stick and sometimes through a diving D-man.

When younger players are first learning deflections, coaches bellow "Stick on the ice!" from the bench. This is still an effective approach in the NHL, as point men use a blade on the ice as a reference point for a shot—"shoot for sticks," as they say.

Given how well NHL goalies cover the bottom of the net, the on-ice deflection isn't always the most effective. Arguably the most desirable shot to deflect is one that comes in waist high, where an offensive player will be ready with his stick and where the goalie can't simply drop to the ice to stop the shot. The puck should travel at a midrange velocity—anything slower and the timing of the play can be completely thrown off. Usually, a player will bat down the puck from that height, turning what might have been a glove save for a netminder into a puck that bounds past their skates into the net.

Again, this isn't blind luck—it's a precision-timed skill play involving multiple teammates.

"You've got to time it so that the puck is arriving at the same time you are," center David Backes told *The Sporting News* in 2012. "You've got to make sure you're taking the goalies' eyes away, because if they can see pucks in this league, they're going to stop them. Then you've got to try to get a piece of it when it comes through. It's an art that's tough to perfect."

Part of that art is knowing where the goalie is anticipating the initial shot is headed. Even though puck deflections happen in a split second, it's actually long enough for a player to get cerebral about the thing.

When a player stands in front of a goalie, screening him from an oncoming shot, he's also sensing where that goalie is looking to track the puck. Depending where his eyes are, the player might let a shot slip by him or deflect it on goal. The goalie's style—if he plays a butterfly style, for example—will also dictate what the player does on the deflection.

Of course, the other factor on any deflection play is the defender standing next to you, attempting to prevent any connection between offensive player and shot from the point.

The physical battle between the two runs the risk of screening the goalie even more than the deflector would have on his own, but it has to be done. Defensemen have to try to box out the offensive player, or at the very least attempt to take his stick away. To that end, it becomes just as much a challenge in timing as it is for a player trying to deflect the puck.

"You've got to get the stick up off the ice," said defenseman Andy Greene to TSN. "It's a tough position, but that's why you have to try to get your position first, and establish position. Usually, if you can establish your own position and something happens, the refs will let it go. If they get position, and you're hooking or trying to get to the guy, that's when they call the penalty, usually."

And that's the tricky part for both players in the battle. The defensive player can't be too aggressive, or run the risk of taking a penalty. The offensive player can't crowd the goalie too much, or else he runs the risk of making some kind of contact and potentially nullifying the goal through a goalie interference penalty.

Then there's the other trick for the offensive player: making sure that a high deflection isn't too high, keeping that stick under the crossbar to keep the goal legal.

It's all about timing, placement, and accuracy. But more than anything, it's about anticipation—where the shot is coming from, what the best deflection might be, and who is trying to stop it.

READY, AIM...OR DON'T

How does one score a goal in hockey?

By overcoming the individuals attempting to prevent it. "Trying to make them [screw] up rather than doing something awesome," as Justin Bourne succinctly puts it.

Two keys to offensive play: creating chaos and executing on chances.

Through their forechecking and their pressure and their cycling and their passing, teams scramble opposing defenses like they're using a whisk. Get them out of their lanes, off of their assignments, and outside of their comfort zones. The objective is to create "soft spaces" around the zone for offensive chances, but it's also essential for giving offensive players the first step.

Defensive coverage is about anticipation, and offensive effectiveness is essentially the art of surprise. Pavel Datsyuk is, perhaps, one of the most innovative stick-handlers in NHL history. Like Gretzky, he's got that sixth hockey sense about what to do and when to do it. It's not planning as much as it is instinct. He knows where he's going before his defender does, and it's nearly impossible to outguess him.

The "Datsyukian Dangle" was entered into the hockey lexicon during his astoundingly good career with the Detroit Red Wings. Datsyuk will skate up ice with the puck. There will be one to four defenders separating him from the goal. At this point, it's like Bruce Lee staring down a group of ninjas—*"What, only four of ya?"*

When he attacks a group of defenders, or when any elite skater does, it's interesting to see who he targets for the deke. In Datsyuk's case, he frequently zeroes in on the player directly in front of him, almost knowing that his puck protection skills are so on point that the other defenders trying to poke it away have no chance. He'll attack that defender, move around him, and fire the puck on goal before the tailing defenders can slow him.

When Pavel Datsyuk is going one-on-one with a defender...well, might as well locate the nearest pair of crutches because someone's about to get their ankles broken. Like the time Datsyuk had Logan Couture in the corner during a Detroit vs. San Jose game. Datsyuk took a pass and headed behind the Sharks' net. On a dime he stopped, reversed course, and appeared to be headed up ice. Again, on a dime, he stopped, bringing his stick to the right, miming like he was going to go behind the net. A millisecond later, Datsyuk had moved his stick from right to left and was skating back up ice.

The entire sequence happened in the time it takes a fly to flap its wings. At the end of it, Logan Couture, professional hockey player, was on his behind having been deked out of his skates.

"The worst part about that? It was my birthday. At least we won the game," Couture wrote on The Players' Tribune in 2014. "Thankfully,

I'm far from the only one to be victimized by Pavel. He has the best hands in the NHL. One little trick he likes to do is stick-handle between a player's tripod—between their feet and stick. He'll even use the net as a prop to make you look dumb."

All the more reason why when you take out your iPhone and ask Siri who the "magic man" is, she'll bring up Pavel Datsyuk's information.

(Seriously, try it. It's hilarious.)

But once a player gets his shot or gets a step around the defense, then they deal with the last, best line of defense: goaltenders.

"Goaltending beats top-notch scoring anytime!" once boasted New York Rangers legend Eddie Giacomin and he wasn't entirely incorrect. Outside of those few players with howitzers for shots that can beat any goalie—Ovechkin, for one—goalies are usually a shooter's tormentor, and not the other way around.

Their increasingly larger bodies—not only do we have some linebackers playing goal in the NHL, their padding can double their size—takes away much of the net. The criticism from opponents about goalies like Henrik Lundqvist "making saves he doesn't actually make" are legion in today's game.

So what's a shooter to do? From long and midrange, it usually means firing the puck at a portion of the net. There's little time to aim; usually, a player is trying to place the puck in the hopes that it'll sneak by or get deflected.

If the chance comes on the rush, a shooter isn't looking for what a goalie's giving them already; they're trying to make the goalie give them something else. So they'll deke and they'll fake and they'll toe drag and they'll try to create chaos in the crease so they can find room to tuck the puck home.

Sometimes the physical attributes of a player factor into his prowess as a goal-scorer. Take Ryan Getzlaf. You'll need a forklift. He's that big.

"Let's start with the obvious—he's a huge man," wrote Couture. "He checks with the best of them. But less obvious is that his reach makes him really very tough to defend because he has the ability to shoot the puck with a ton of power from out wide, which changes the angle and makes it extremely difficult for the goalie to pick up the puck."

Not every player is blessed with those natural gifts. So the majority of NHLers have to rely on their craftiness to excel.

Another facet of the art of deception is the release point of shots. Slightly changing the angle of a shot will force the goalie to reset, and in turn might open up some part of his body that wasn't previously a target. This change-up can also create rebound chances in front.

Speaking of rebounds: slap shots remain the most satisfying way to fire the puck at the goalie, if not the most effective.

The *Toronto Star*, in 2013, released a story of all 6,949 goals scored in the NHL in the 2011–12 season:

"The wrist shot proved the most deadly, accounting for 3,369 goals, 48.5 percent of all goals. Shots from the 11-to-15 foot range accounted for 1,577 goals (22.7) percent with the six-to-10 foot range a close second (1,426, 8.5 percent). Almost as many wrist shots—842—were scored in the 11-to-15 foot range as all the slap shots (892) combined from all distances. There is one basic area where a goalie is more susceptible than anywhere else: stick side. Sure, the goalie's blocker is there, and so is his paddle. But based on the percentages, it's where a majority of goals are scored, especially low stick side."

That said, there are hockey gods who can drop the hammer on a booming slap shot to score; the rest of the mortals have to use their repertoire—and some happy accidents off bodies in front of the goal—to put one past a goalie.

WHERE GOALS WERE SCORED IN 2011–12

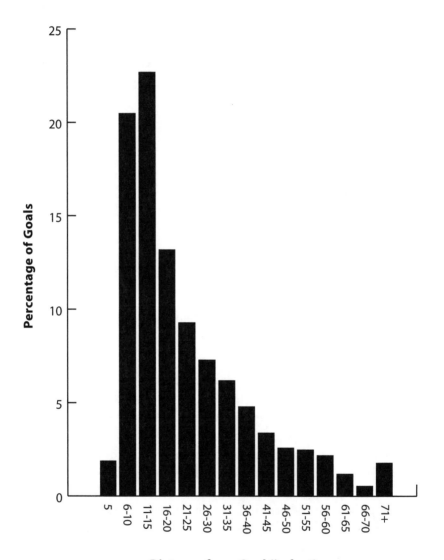

Distance from Goal (in feet)

(Source: *Toronto Star*)

Wayne Gretzky, by the way? Not a mortal.

His vision as a playmaker was unparalleled. His accuracy as a shooter, however, was born out of knowing his limitations, which is something that even the Great One had to face.

For Gretzky, that meant shot velocity. He used a stick that traded power on his shots for accuracy.

"My stick was so stiff that my accuracy every single day was pretty pinpoint. So I couldn't shoot as hard as other guys, but I knew exactly where I was shooting it," he told TSN in 2014.

Mortals usually only experience this on a breakaway.

MANO A MANO

So how can a shooter beat a goalie on a breakaway?

Deception.

No matter if the shooter is attempting to open up a goalie's five-hole (so named because it's the fifth scoring zone after the four corners) or going glove side, there will be some type of deke or fake to give the netminder a moment of indecision. For some shooters, it's like trying to cross a guy over in basketball, faking one way and going another. For other shooters, it's about trying to catch the goalie off-guard with the timing of the shot.

"For me, it's about trying to watch what the goalie does," said Edmonton Oilers winger Jordan Eberle. "If I see the goalie is out pretty far, I usually have a deke move planned. Usually my backhand. If he's back, tighter to the net, I think it's easier to get a shot off."

Again, this is easier said than done. Goalie coaching for breakaways has them positionally sound, matching the speed of the shooter and waiting until the last moment to react so as not to open up any holes.

Watch the goalie on a breakaway: unless he decides he needs to challenge the shooter, he's simply going to wait out the chance more often than not, knowing there's a better chance the shooter pumps the puck off his pads or wide of the net than scoring a goal.

The antidote for the patient netminder is to make him move. This can usually be accomplished by coming at him at an angle.

"It's good to get a different angle, like coming in wide," said Eberle. "You always want to have two things ready: a shot if he's in tight, or a deke move."

Of course, it helps if you have a move they simply can't stop.

Like Frans Nielsen's backhand, which sticks inside the roof of the net like peanut butter in one's mouth.

"I keep wondering every summer if [goalies] are going to catch on to me," Nielsen told *Newsday*. "It's fun to still have success doing it."

Like T.J Oshie's legendary move—deke to the five-hole, go forehand to backhand to forehand in a millisecond, and then tuck the puck behind a baffled goalie—that defeated the Russians in the 2014 Olympics and landed Oshie on *The TODAY Show*.

"I come in slow, go from right to left, and then cut to the middle. I pull the puck to my forehand and I leave it there. And then I just flick my wrist a little bit, throw it five-hole, and hope it goes in," said Oshie.

Simple and easy, and yet the Russians couldn't stop it if Vladimir Putin drove a tank onto the ice and parked it in front of the goal. Shirtless, of course.

Those are the exceptions. Breakaways are a goalie's moment to shine or blow it, but mostly shine. They have the advantage, no matter who the shooter is.

That Gretzky fellow we've referred to in this chapter? He was 2-for-6 in penalty shots during his career.

What a hack.

CHAPTER 4

THE DEFENSEMEN

Ah, defensemen.

"What's the perception of the position? That the slow kids got put back there."

That's Aaron Ward, who played 15 seasons in the NHL, winning the Stanley Cup with the Detroit Red Wings and the Carolina Hurricanes. You'd think a guy who played with Nicklas Lidstrom, a hockey demigod who became a Hall of Fame defenseman subtly nicknamed "The Perfect Human," wouldn't feel the need to defend the virtues of his chosen position. And yet…

"The vast majority of the time, you put the slow kid back on 'D' because he doesn't have the offensive skill and you just go to the lowest common denominator," said Ward, now a broadcaster for TSN in Canada. "The thinking goes, 'If you can't skate, maybe you can stop people.'"

But rather than a collection of hands-of-stone-and-skates-to-match athletes on the blue line, Ward sees this as the most cerebral position in hockey.

Yes, even more than the guy who figures out the salary cap space.

"It's a smart man's position," Ward said. "You can extend your career based on your knowledge. It's not always the skill that keeps you there.

If you're smart enough to get a mental Rolodex on some guys, you know what they're going to do during games."

Just like goalies, defensemen remember tendencies. You may have heard that for all of his goal-scoring prowess, Alex Ovechkin doesn't exactly have a magician's chest of tricks as an offensive player. When Ward would defend him, he knew the play would go one of two ways: Ovechkin would drive wide of the defender, or fake the drive wide and come to the middle. Simple, predictable, and defendable…as long as the defenseman doesn't overplay his hand. Lunge at the puck, attempt to poke if off his stick, and Ovechkin blazes past you like a comet.

"Playing forward is a reactionary game. You react to what's given to you. Defense is an action game. You're always reading what's going on. Forward is very instinctual. Playing defense is very much like a quarterback, checking off on receivers," is how Ward sees it.

But unlike a quarterback, the objective usually isn't crossing the goal line.

ANGLES AND CONTROL

My favorite line from *Raiders of the Lost Ark*?

Glad you (probably wouldn't have) asked (but I'll go ahead and mention it anyway).

It's when the villainous Belloq utters to our hero, "Doctor Jones…again we see there is nothing you can possess which I cannot take away."

This is essentially the mantra for defensemen. They want to take away a scoring chance. They want take away the puck an attacking player possesses. But in order to do both, they have to begin by taking away space. The essential task for a defenseman in his own end is to not allow an offensive player room to create, and to force that player into doing things he doesn't want to do with the puck.

Two terms you'll hear constantly when watching defensemen ply their trade: "gap control" and an "active stick."

Gap control refers to the space between an offensive player and a defenseman. Watch the defending player. Notice how much space there is between him and the offensive player as the attacker moves toward the goal. At first, it'll likely be a stick's length, allowing the defender to quickly react with his lumber if the puck-carrier attempts a shot or a pass.

He'll match the attacker's stride and speed, so he can't be beaten by a sudden move to the outside. He'll angle the shooter, taking away his shooting lane by positioning himself between the attacker and the goal. The key, as you'll see on basically every rush, is for the defenseman to keep his outside shoulder lined up with the shooter's inside shoulder, preventing a clear shot or path to the net.

As the play reaches the top of the circles, the gap closes. The defenseman challenges the shooter so the attacking player basically has to travel through him to get to the goal. If he's guarding a player without the puck, he's closed in to take away a passing option.

The aforementioned "active stick"—besides being an essential achievement in the Eddie Olczyk NBC broadcaster drinking game—describes what the defenseman needs to do with his twig when taking on an attacker. It should always be on the ice, always in motion, always seeking to be as close to the shooter's blade as possible.

The stick becomes vital when a defenseman is trying to block a pass. You'll see it every game: a player drops down to one knee and puts the shaft of his stick on the ice in an effort to take away a passing lane. It's an effective move…provided it doesn't put him woefully out of position.

"If you have your stick on the ice, it's just one more object for players to pass. Even if you're away from the puck or not the guy right on the puck, you try and keep your stick on the ice. You might get lucky with

Q. What are the differences between left and right defensemen?

A: It's always been a conundrum why there isn't a formal designation for left and right defensemen, like there is for wingers. The only inkling of an answer is that they switch sides so often during play that the designation is fleeting, but it's not as if the same can't be said of wingers.

The difference, typically, is handedness. A right-handed defenseman playing the right side is able to use his stick on the forehand to play the puck along the boards. A left-handed player has the disadvantage of playing the same puck on his backhand.

Some coaches are obsessed with having uniformity—"on-hand" players on both sides—but it's more an ideal than something a general manager is going to mandate for his lineup.

But playing on your "off hand" (i.e., lefty on the right side) is much more beneficial on offense. Zdeno Chara loves to get off his one-timer as a right defenseman with a left-handed shot. On the power play, handedness can be important. The angles provided by having a right-handed shot on the left point and a lefty on the right side are ideal. Look no further than Al MacInnis (723 career power-play points) and Gary Suter (477), one of the greatest power-play tandems in NHL history. They fit that template.

It also depends on the system a team plays. Back in the days of Detroit's Left Wing Lock, the left defenseman had a middle-of-the-ice role that could be handled by a righty or a lefty.

your stick," defenseman Adam McQuaid told the *Boston Globe*. "If you have one hand on your stick, you're not going to be as strong as when you have two hands. You need to get in and have a little more strength. Maybe lean on the guy with the stick. It happens quick. So you have to read what situation you're in."

This skill comes especially handy in defending an odd-man rush. Watch a 2-on-1 break. The defender has to make a split-second determination on which player is the more dangerous option for his goalie. If that means taking away a pass across the middle, you'll see defensive bodies sprawled over the passing lane. If that means disrupting a potential shot, you'll still see a defender try and take away that other option to better give his goalie a clear chance to save the shot.

"It's all reactive," said Ward. "You're trying to delay as much as you can to get numbers back to help out. Don't give them primary scoring chances. Give them what you want them to have and nothing more."

Of course, the stick can also be used for more…nefarious purposes.

Defensemen are essentially like tollbooth collectors: they impede your journey until you pay the price, and then you go through the stick to be on your merry way.

Unless of course you have EZ-PASS, which for the purposes of this comparison was NHL game flow right after the 2005–06 lockout when anything resembling obstruction was whistled.

Gradually that subsided, and the NHL returned to its comfort zone of low-scoring games and defensemen slowing down goal-scorers with their lumber. Hooking, steering, tangling…it happens every game and it's only called situationally, because otherwise we'd have five-hour games with 10 power plays on each side. Which would, in theory, increase scoring, but really make going to the games difficult for parents on weeknights. ("Honey, call the sitter—Subban just got *another* hooking minor.")

There's more stick-work from defensemen worth noting here, namely those jabs around an opponent's gloves in an attempt to force a turnover.

One of Hall of Fame defenseman Larry Robinson's favorite moves was a little flick of the wrist with his stick that would disrupt the puck-carrier.

"That's what you were taught when you were little because everybody's not big and has the strength to be able to get under a guy's stick and lift it. You just kind of tap him on the hands. That's how the little guys used to get away with it. Now it's a slash or a hook," he lamented to the *San Jose Mercury News*. "If you tomahawk him, that's different, but if a guy is going up the wall and you just give him a little tap on the hand where he loses the puck, to me that's not a penalty. To me that's a great hockey play."

Yes, the tomahawk is a bit different. And the fact is that any contact around the gloves in today's NHL results in the puck-carrier throwing his mitts in the air like he has suddenly spontaneously combusted in an effort to elaborately draw a penalty.

But embellishment works both ways for defensemen. One of my pet peeves is when a D-man decides to protect the puck by turning his numbers in the face of an onrushing forechecker in an effort to draw a boarding call on what would otherwise be a routine check.

"Some of the rules I agree they had to make. But I look at it now to where guys, with the rules they have now, guys take advantage of them," said Robinson. "There'll be a race for the puck and a guy'll just turn his back because now you're not allowed to hit from behind. It is a physical game and there is contact, so shouldn't it kind of be a two-way street?"

In theory? Yes.

SHOT-BLOCKING

The old adage is that teams that lead the league in "hits" shouldn't actually celebrate that achievement. After all, you can only hit the guy with the puck if in fact you don't possess it yourself.

The same theory holds for shot-blocking, which has become a prevalent part of a defenseman's game.

"If you're blocking shots it means the puck is in your zone a lot. When you're a shot-blocking team, you never get it back," said coach Ken Hitchcock.

That might be difficult to hear for the players who sacrifice their bodies on a game-to-game basis, hitting the ice with reckless abandon so someone can fire a piece of frozen rubber at them at around 90 mph.

"Imagine taking the rubber mallet in your dad's tool shed, putting it in the freezer for a few hours, then getting hit as hard as you can with it. That's how it feels," defenseman John-Michael Liles told the *Charlotte Observer*.

So why do so many defensemen block shots? According to defenseman Rob Scuderi, it might be because there are more opportunities to do so.

"I think maybe you've seen an increase in the number of blocked shots because more of the emphasis on the offensive end is shooting the puck," Scuderi told the *Los Angeles Times*. "If you're in the right position, you'll probably get a block. I'm not sure what the number would be, but I'm sure if you took the shots plus the shots attempted you'd have a pretty high number. The chances are 20 to 25 percent of those are getting blocked. It's about being in the right position and hopefully some hit you."

Those pucks usually do hit defensemen, which is why shot-blocking is effective: if the goal of defensive play is to interrupt the flow of offensive play, then choreographed defensive bodies sliding into the shooting lanes is quite the disruption.

But the reason they block so many shots is also thanks to science and coaching. Over the years, the techniques for shot-blocking have improved dramatically, as players rarely attempt to block shots by sliding skates-first into a blast as they once might have. Instead, they drop to one knee, using their leg and their stick to attempt to stop the puck.

"The way I was taught, unless you're desperate, you don't want to slide because you get out of position," ECHL defenseman Dyson Stevenson said. "They can easily go around you, especially the smart defensemen here."

That's good coaching; the science can be found in the equipment the players wear that protects them a might bit better than it did 20 years ago. The players who block the most shots wear extra padding in their gloves and extensions on their shin pads. The skate protection technology has improved by leaps as well, with Kevlar boot casings preserving the ankles of the shot-blockers.

Of course, like many other safety features in the NHL, this one comes down to whether the players want to sacrifice a little weight for a whole lotta safety in a skate protector.

It used to be a specialty amongst players, but now everyone's expected to be able to block a shot. The rise of it as a tactic for all teams—the point where it's included in "death of hockey" laments as a smotherer of offense—coincides with the new rules established during the 2005 lockout.

The ostensive end of obstruction with those rules meant increased offensive output for teams, creating more scoring chances. No longer able to set picks at the blue line or to wrap up attacking players like a boa constrictor, defensemen turned to shot-blocking as the next-best way to take away what those shooters possessed.

The best way to approach the skill? Don't think about its repercussions.

"If you're thinking about that, you're not going to block any shots, because that's always going to be in the back of your head," Rangers defenseman Dan Girardi said. "You just got to react to the play. There are always risks with anything. Anything can happen on that ice."

No guts (or temporary insanity), no glory. Shot-blockers are always among the biggest cult heroes among fans—think of the Gregory

Campbell mania, when the Bruins' fourth-liner broke his leg on a blocked Evgeni Malkin shot but remained on the ice to finish his penalty-killing stint. Seriously, sonnets were being written. Or Dropkick Murphys songs. One of the two.

It's not just fans who appreciate it, either. "I like to come to the bench after blocking a shot and all the guys are really appreciative of that," Stevenson said. "Especially the goaltenders. If you're in the way, you've

Q. Is it true that defense presents the biggest learning curve for young NHL skaters?

A: Wingers have it easiest, that's for sure: skate hard, head down, don't turn the puck over, and try your best to hit the net, kid.

Centers have it harder. I remember talking to Matt Duchene of the Colorado Avalanche about the learning curve for a young man in the middle, and he told me that the defensive responsibilities in your own end increase exponentially from junior hockey to pro hockey.

But the largest learning curve is on defense, by far. Not only are you learning systems you haven't played before, you're feeling out how to act and react as a defenseman on the pro level. You simply can't take the chances you did in junior, or else you'll be eaten alive by elite talent. As the brilliant former No. 1 overall pick Aaron Ekblad did with the Florida Panthers in 2014–15, you rely heavily on your veteran defense partner for support.

Ekblad, like Victor Hedman before him, was blessed with some size when entering the league. But while a forward can get by as a beanpole that's 150 pounds soaking wet, a defenseman needs to develop physically to handle the human wrecking balls hurled at him every game.

Defensemen tend to stay in the minors longer and percolate for a reason.

got to block it or it's probably going to go in the net. So I try to do that. Obviously it doesn't feel great, but that's why we wear the equipment."

Well, everyone wears the equipment. It's just a matter of how hard you get hit.

WHEN TO HIT

The true joy in watching the NHL's best hitters isn't in the impact but in the anticipation.

The Red Wings' Niklas Kronwall is a good example. He spent 11 years laying out opponents without a suspension until 2015. Rare is the individual in sports whose name is turned into a verb, but "Kronwalling" was real and it was spectacularly painful.

The setup: a player will have the puck, usually near the boards, usually in his own end. He'll pass it up ice. Kronwall will then rocket in from the blue line and explode into a hit—his skates coming off the ice frequently, but on impact. Down goes the foe, but rarely did the referee's arm go up.

"I haven't seen many guys better, over the years, of being a bait-and-switch type of guy," said NBC's Eddie Olczyk. "You know when he's on the ice. He's highlighted in team meetings, his name is on the dry-erase board. You have to know exactly where he is. But when you take a quick look when you have the puck, you see him accelerating backward. But all he's doing is getting ready to open, pivot, and knock you in there.

"A lot of his hits are right on the line. But they're good, hard, violent hits."

A devastating legal hit is something to behold—a symphony of timing, velocity, and, in the modern NHL, targeting.

I became a fan during an era when a hit to the head was seen as a tactical strike, and, to the end, Scott Stevens was a cruise missile. The former Devils captain would catch opponents with their heads down or time his hits so his shoulder would connect with another player's noggin. His hits on Slava Kozlov and Paul Kariya in the Stanley Cup Finals in 1995 and 2003, respectively, were simply brutal and intrinsically game-changing; ditto his masterpiece, the hit he put on Eric Lindros of the Flyers during the Eastern Conference Final in 2000 that knocked Lindros out and helped the Devils to victory.

In hindsight, these hits are barbaric—then again, they used to let you smoke on airplanes, too. Stripped of that disregard for head trauma, they've every bit the marvels of timing and anticipation that Kronwall's hits are.

So when is the right time to unleash hell? A few factors:

Staying Within the Play
The most basic question on a hit isn't necessarily the "how" but the "when and where." Is the check going to end up making a difference on a play? Is it one that, depending on the result of the hit, could take you out of position, or leave you behind the play? Body control is the key here, for recovery after a check.

Throwing a Check Instead of a Hit
The game's best hitters aren't just running into opponents like two people trying to enter and leave a crowded elevator. You put your shoulder down and find a low center of gravity as you collide with the other guy. This is to make the hit as effective as possible, but also to ensure that you're not the one getting injured.

Try Not to Do Something Stupid
Easier said than done in a game played at this velocity and in a league where, with appalling frequency, players being hit are doing things to draw penalties, like turning their numbers to a hitter along the boards. Committing to the hit is paramount, or else you run the risk of everyone involved getting hurt. But sometimes recognizing the situation

is just as paramount. (As well as understanding how not to deliver a hit; for example, catching air like a ski-jumper before making contact.)

GETTING OFFENSIVE ON DEFENSE

We've spent a lot of time talking about the home-run hits, but in reality most checks are singles.

Checking along the boards is a fundamental skill, but it's also one of the game's most underrated battles. You'll hear terms like "mucking and grinding," and this is what they're talking about: defensive players trying to pin offensive players against the boards, and those offensive players fighting through it.

An effective check is going to be a combination of lower and upper body positioning. Watch the defenseman's lower body—legs wide, low center of gravity, digging his skate into the ice to put as much pressure on the puck-carrier as possible. At the same time, he's keeping his shoulders square to the boards and using his chest to pin his opponent against the glass.

It's all about trying to separate player from puck, and trying to slow down an offensive attack, which is what pays the bills if you're a defenseman.

Unless, of course, you're not an immobile pylon and can bring the offense, too.

The new rules in 2005–06 changed several facets of a defenseman's job, including his role in the offense.

When the red line was "taken out" and two-line passes were allowed, the stretch pass became a greater weapon for defensemen. If Aaron Ward likens defensemen to NFL quarterbacks, then this is like throwing the deep ball: a pass from a defender's own zone to a streaking offensive player. Miss the target, and it's either a turnover or an icing. Hit the target, and the result could be a lit goal light (and a nice secondary assist for the defenseman who started the breakout).

We've covered the prowess of defensemen in their own end, but haven't explored how important they are for team offense. So let's put a fine point on it, shall we?

Puck-moving defensemen are the single most valuable commodity in professional hockey.

Don't confuse "valuable" with "precious." A No. 1 center and a 70-start goalie are more precious, in the sense they're as rare as the Hope Diamond. But if you're a defenseman looking for a contract on the open market and you handle the puck better than you defend it, you're going to get money thrown at you like you're in one of those glass boxes with the dollar bills floating around.

Puck-moving defensemen get you out of trouble in your own end, and transition to offense in the neutral zone. Puck-moving defensemen usually possess the heck out of the puck, allowing for teams to comfortably change lines. Puck-moving defensemen generate offense, either by setting up the breakouts; firing a shot through traffic at the opposite blue line; or flat out joining the rush.

It creates that vital ingredient for an offensive chance, which is confusion on the opposing defense. The defense does a good job on marking opposing forwards; throw a trailing defenseman into the mix and suddenly it's scrambled eggs instead of an omelet.

Whether or not a defenseman jumps up into the play depends largely on two factors.

First is the play itself, and the puck possession for the attacking forwards. A defenseman will join the rush as he breaks out of his own zone and skates through the neutral zone; whether or not he fully commits to joining the rush deep will be determined around the attacking blue line.

The other factor is whether the defenseman has the green light to join the rush. A defenseman like Erik Karlsson is allowed to act like a fourth forward, because Erik Karlsson is a Swedish offensive freak machine. Few players have his recovery speed should he get caught up ice, but many elite point-scoring defensemen have the hockey sense to know when to dabble in the dark arts of offensive hockey. Most coaches demand that their defensemen skate their rumps off to get into the offensive flow as a "late-wave option," giving the forwards an option below the blue line and before the dots.

If a defenseman "activates" offensively, it's imperative that a forward be aware that he may need to provide coverage at the top of the zone if his defenseman pinches and there's a "handoff" of the puck between the two or if the defenseman cuts to the middle for an open look.

But mostly, a defenseman's contributions in the offensive zone are limited to shots from the blue line that he tries to pinball off players and past the goalie. (Or that are blocked by a defenseman on the other team, in a cruel twist of fate.)

The key to effective point play is reading the defense. The first option for a defenseman on offense is to load up the cannon and blast away, but if that's not there it comes down to three other options: feed the other point, attempt a pass to a forward down low, or send the puck deep into the corner in the hopes that his forwards have a step on the defense.

To the offensive defenseman go the spoils. A quick check of the highest-paid defensemen reveals a collection of players who put up as many goals as they prevent. And yet there's a notion from some defensemen, like Torey Krug of the Boston Bruins, that being labeled an "offensive defenseman" is somehow being labeled a one-dimensional player.

"I wanted to become a top-four defenseman and get rid of that 'offensive defenseman' title," he said.

ILL COMMUNICATION

As we mentioned, the goal for offensive players is utter chaos. The goal for defensemen is to combat that chaos with structure, confidence, and, above all else, communication.

Which was something Aaron Ward would sometimes struggle with, during his days with the Bruins.

"I had Zdeno Chara go batshit," he said. "I have A.D.D. We'd be on a faceoff and I would be looking around, checking out where the popcorn guy was. But [Chara] wants communication. He wants to know where people are going to be. So he would lose his marbles about me sometimes."

And you don't want a Slovakian man mountain losing his marbles on you.

Communication has to happen. It has to happen when the puck is dumped in, as one defenseman shouts out instructions to his partner, who has his back to the play: "Quick up!" or "Reverse!"

Granted, some veteran pairings can sense what the other is going to do without a large amount of yapping, which is why they're veteran pairings. But overall, D-men are constantly talking to each other…and especially to their goalies.

Or at least attempting to.

Imagine being in a concert band where the conductor just sort of stood there, zoned out, never cueing the French horns. Well, that's just how some goalies like to conduct their business. Tim Thomas, Vezina winner for the Boston Bruins? Not a talker. Cam Ward, Conn Smythe winner for the Carolina Hurricanes? Like Quentin Tarantino after a Red Bull.

Defensemen want a goalie who talks, instructs, and acts like a general back there. But more than anything, they want a goalie who can be another defenseman, who can handle the puck.

(An aside: at this point we should mention the damned trapezoid, the area behind the net that extends 28 feet wherein the goalie is not allowed to play the puck. I'm against it, as it's a rule that basically punishes elite skill. Some goalies play the puck as well as forwards and they can be the best defense against a forecheck. There are also feckless fumblehands who would make a hash out of a puck in deep and give away a goal.

(But the trapezoid is actually an affront to player safety. Allowing goalies to play the puck would lead to fewer plays on which a defenseman is rendered defenseless against an onrushing forechecker, attempting to play the puck and protect himself while contorting into an Auntie Anne's pretzel along the end boards.

(Yet in the modern NHL, the trapezoid might not even matter. The lack of obstruction at the blue line means that forecheckers get back on the puck quickly, which means many goalies aren't going to venture out of their crease to play it anyway. Still, it's stupid and we hate it. Moving on…)

OK, what defensemen *really, really* want out of their goalies is for them to be active participants in the game plan. A goalie who pays attention to systems, who sits in on pre-scouting meetings, who understands where his defensemen are going to be in the zone and where he needs to keep the puck from going.

Where does a goalie want the puck not to go? Behind him. Which is why goalies and defensemen work in concert when there's a screen at the doorstep of the crease.

Watch the battles in front of the net. Defensemen try to physically move forwards from the crease, but more than that they're trying to take an opponent's stick out of the equation so there are no deflections, all while not screening one's own goalie.

Forwards around the net have become more tactical, frequently looking for opportunities around the net rather than standing like monoliths in front of it. Defensemen have to match that positioning, but also need to be ready to transition should the play go the other way.

If you've detected a theme here, it's that changes to the NHL rules over time have managed to hurt the effectiveness of defensemen. It's not different in front of the net, where back in the day defenders could take…ahem…certain liberties with their opponents.

"It used to be an absolute [expletive] massacre at the net," recalled Ward. "We were like lumberjacks. I used to break sticks on guys all the time."

It's a practice generally frowned upon today.

IT'S ALL YOUR FAULT

Forwards have it easy. If they screw up, there's always another shift and another shot and a chance at the ultimate redemption, which is a goal.

Goalies have it slightly worse. They're a one-person show, so the blame is focused. But they also can be let off the hook if the team in front of them plays poorly, and there's always sympathy for the volume of shots they face.

Defensemen…they can't win. Their position is one of nuance, one that rarely results in a play where you can palpably point to something and say, "This thing happened because of a spectacular play by the defenseman!" They're a bit like referees in the sense that the less you hear their names, the better they're doing.

But when they fail to do their job…well, someone will notice.

Aaron Ward had a YouTube video. It's not his, but one that someone created about him. It was a 2009 game against the New Jersey Devils, when Ward was a member of the Carolina Hurricanes. It's 71 seconds of the worst shift of his life: three turnovers, one near penalty, one called penalty, and more than a minute of frantically chasing Devils players around like they owed him money. The only time he was in position might have been on the faceoff.

Insult to injury: the fan who uploaded it added little cartoon bubbles that acted as Ward's internal monologue. *LOL I just cross-checked someone, why can't I get a penalty...*

They're the slow guys, the dumb guys, and the guys whose mistakes make great viral videos.

Ah, defensemen.

"A forward can kind of escape criticism for a very long time. You're not glaringly off. But if a defenseman's bad, he's [expletive] horrible," said Ward.

CHAPTER 5

VERY SPECIAL TEAMS

The best power play in NHL history, as far back as the stats currently measure, belonged to the 1977–78 Montreal Canadiens.

They converted 31.88 percent of their power-play opportunities, as Hall of Famer Guy Lafleur netted 15 goals and 21 assists on the man advantage—numbers that would have made him the fifth *overall leading scorer* on the putrid Washington Capitals team that season.

The previous season, with much of the same personnel?

It was 24.89 percent. Still stellar, but not historic.

The worst power play in NHL history? That would be the 1997–98 Tampa Bay Lightning, sporting a nearly hilarious conversion rate of 9.35 percent. But to paraphrase Brian Fontana of *Anchorman*: "Nine point three five percent of the time, it works every time…"

The immortal Paul Ysebaert led the team with 15 power-play points, which helped balance out the minus-43 (!) he sported at even strength. The Islanders' Ziggy Palffy, the league's leading power-play scorer that season with 17 tallies, had as many goals as the top four Lightning players on the power play combined.

The next season, with the addition of old war horse Wendel Clark and 18-year-old rookie Vinny Lecavalier? It jumped to 13.87 percent, which was still below the league average but not an abject disaster.

The point is that special teams are both the most reliable and unreliable variable in hockey, year to year.

They're reliable in the sense that a team that excels at both is probably going to do quite well, and a team that does both poorly is going to be a steaming pile of dung. The Canadiens won the Stanley Cup in 1978; the Lightning somehow crammed in two 16-game winless streaks into the same putrid season, finishing with a 1–12–1 streak as well.

They're unreliable because they're fickle. The percentages are a good indicator, but every great power play has a clunker of a game and every great PK gives up a goal in a key situation. Overreliance on one or the other is a fool's errand—especially when you consider how the number of power-play chances evaporate when the playoffs arrive.

That said, special teams can be the difference between making and missing those playoffs, especially the power play.

It helps when you have an Alex Ovechkin to deploy.

HE'S GOT THE POWER

Alex Ovechkin is the Russian goofball who happens to also be one of the most lethal snipers in NHL history, and especially on the power play. He's the Washington Capitals' franchise leader in power-play goals for a career and a single season. Having averaged more than 17 goals per season on the man advantage, Ovechkin seems poised to assault the all-time NHL record for power-play goals set by Dave Andreychuk (274).

Andreychuk played from 1982 through 2006 with six different teams, and is the antithesis of Ovechkin on the power play. He was a garbage collector: he used a large frame (6-foot-4, 220 pounds) to plant himself in front of opposing goalies, and then either watch the puck bounce off of him or knock home point-blank rebounds for goals.

Like many snipers, Ovechkin's home is on the half wall near the left faceoff circle, to the right of the goalie. It's as much his office as behind the net was Gretzky's. The truly great scorers have the unique ability to get their shot off in a variety of ways depending on the quality of the pass and what the defense gives them. And everyone knows where the puck is going, or at least where the team on the man advantage is trying to place it.

But that's the beauty of having an elite goal-scorer on your power play: he works just as effectively as a decoy as he does the primary conduit for offense.

"If teams take me away or a guy is just standing in front of me all the time, then different guys [will] score goals," Ovechkin said. "The power play is not about me. I don't have to score. Of course, if I have the chance to score then I'm going to put the puck in the net."

Watch what penalty-killers do with a sniper. If they overcommit and try to take his space away, watch how the power play reacts in getting other options open. Specifically with Ovechkin, when he notices the PK is shadowing him, he'll fade deeper and deeper into the zone to draw the defenders with him. That opens up a point shot for his defenseman, with Ovechkin now lying in wait for a rebound attempt.

Of course, it's great to have a finisher…assuming he's got something to finish.

MECHANICS OF THE SCORING MACHINE

"It doesn't always start with the skill you have on the ice, if you follow the steps," said Buffalo Sabres coach Dan Bylsma, who once coached some of the most skilled players in the NHL on the power play when he was in Pittsburgh. "It starts with the breakout."

Q: Why not just use five forwards on the power play?

A: The short answer is that it's not necessary. Most teams have at least one puck-moving defenseman who can act as a "fifth forward" while also having a modicum of defensive responsibility.

But why hasn't a team loaded with talent up front decided to go all forwards on the power play? Truthfully, because no one's excelled at it yet.

Rangers coach John Tortorella flirted with the idea in the 2011 preseason, with center Brad Richards as the power-play quarterback. But it never made it past the test stages. Richards was the kind of two-way forward you would need to manage the blue line on a five-forward power play. Like dynamic puck-moving defensemen, many teams have a center like that, but not all of them.

Kyle Dubas, assistant general manager of the Toronto Maple Leafs, believes that the "best way to play the game" is something that's constantly changing. "Might we see the abolishment of defensemen one day? Will we see teams go with four forwards in overtime?" he asks.

Perhaps. And if four forwards start winning teams OT points, it would be just a matter of time before five forwards get a regular crack at the power play.

Around 85 percent of the time, a team emerges from its own zone with an all-five-man power-play breakout. Everyone has a route to take. Everyone has to skate hard. Each puck-carrier will have at least two passing options through the neutral zone, provided those players stay in their lanes.

The next step is what to do at the blue line. If it's a carry in, you might see teams slide a forward across the blue line to attempt to keep the defense honest, creating some space for the zone entry.

Again, the key is to give the puck-carrier options. If the pass is down the wing from a defenseman to a forward, that forward should have an option behind the net, one near the slot, and the defenseman who started the play back at the blue line.

Once possession is established, the power play starts churning like dough in a mixer. There are a few basic keys to any power play:

1. Constant motion
2. Traffic in front
3. Recovery options

The first one should be the easiest, and yet many teams are guilty of being flat-footed in the attacking zone. Giving everyone a touch on the power play helps keep the unit engaged...provided someone ends the passing drill by succumbing to the idiots in the stands who scream "SHOOOOOOT!" (Seriously, people: don't scream "Shoot!" Save your breath for booing when your guys inevitably shoot right into an opposing player's skates, and the puck is cleared.)

Traffic in front is easier said than established. It's a battle between a forward and a defenseman to clear the goalie's lines of sight and to take away any scoring chances that forward might generate on a rebound. This dynamic has changed over the years.

"I used to crack the guys with lumber, and they'd slash you back," recalled former NHL defenseman Aaron Ward. "But now defensemen play more positional and less 'grunt.' So now the defenseman isn't just trying to take away the offensive guy, but is trying to get ready to transition to offense himself."

That leads to the third key: recovery options. Typically, a shot on goal is going to have a player around the crease to collect it, as well as two players on the flanks who are ready to crash the crease or chase the puck to the boards to corral it. Again, the players have routes they need to follow—a forward going to a certain spot for a safety-valve pass, a defenseman pinching the wall near the blue line.

If it works, possession is maintained and the power play continues to generate chances against an exhausted defense—but a defense that, nonetheless, kills the vast majority of the power plays it faces.

KILL! KILL! KILL!

From 2003 through 2015, nine of 12 Stanley Cup champions had a penalty kill above the league average and a power play below it. This speaks to their strength at 5-on-5, but it also speaks to how sound defensive teams are always going to get the better of good offensive teams because, to quote Dark Helmet from *Spaceballs*, good is dumb.

But it also speaks to how much easier it is to kill a penalty than it is to score a power-play goal. And, frankly, how much more fun it is to suppress offense than to orchestrate it.

"It's a thinking game, and it's a challenge. You're a guy down. You're not expected to do anything. And then you get the opportunity to make a play and it's just kind of fun to have an extra challenge," said forward Tyler Johnson of the Tampa Bay Lightning. "It's a chess match out there. Everyone's trying to get open, set up plays. You have a split second to decide what they're trying, and then disrupt it. You're trying to figure out what they're doing, and they're doing the exact same thing. It's pretty cool."

Aaron Ward echoed something commonplace for many players on the PK: it's about the grunts getting one over on the star players.

"Most times you have a skill player or two out there on the penalty kill, but there's a pride that goes into the penalty kill. It's oftentimes the biggest factor in the game," he said. "When they take it across the red line to the blue line, and they can't get the puck into the zone, and the crowd is all anxious…it's the greatest. It's a grassroots game and that's a grassroots situation. They have five guys. You have four. And you overcome adversity? That's the nature and makeup of a hockey player.

"And in practice, if we could make it where the power play couldn't score a single goal, all the prima donnas had to spend the rest of the day thinking about it. It was a badge of honor. If you could make sure you kept them off the board, against all the plugs they were playing against, it was the greatest."

What should you watch on the penalty kill?

The Faceoff

The key to the kill, since every PK begins with one and since gaining possession of the puck off the draw can cut into the shorthanded time significantly. Typically, players on the kill are going to be more aggressive in trying to gain possession right off the draw by having forwards and defensemen crowd the box. But the key to the shorthanded faceoff, especially in the defensive zone, is to send the puck to an area where one of the other three killers can locate it, possess it, and clear it.

Pressuring the Zone Entry

If the penalty kill can successfully stand up the puck-carrier, or force a turnover for a clear down ice, it can subtract huge chunks of seconds from the man advantage. More importantly, it can find time to make personnel changes, while the power play will generally keep the same unit out to regroup and attack. Shifts on the penalty kill should, ideally, be around 30 seconds.

Penalty kills will typically have one forward who pressures the puck-carrier and a defenseman who attempts to contain the half-boards. The other forward will chase pucks to the corners while also establishing himself as a potential passing option on a turnover. The other defenseman will go to the net and establish a presence there.

Containment Inside the Zone

Once the power play begins to establish itself in the attacking zone, the penalty kill begins to actively contain and prevent chances. Watch the positioning of the killers: are they trying to take away passing lanes?

STANLEY CUP POWER PLAY

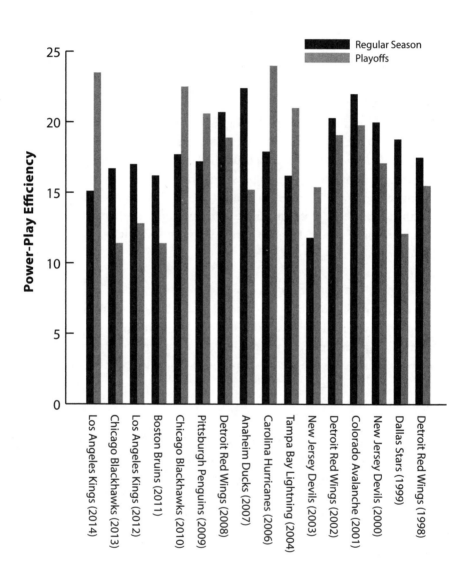

STANLEY CUP PENALTY KILL

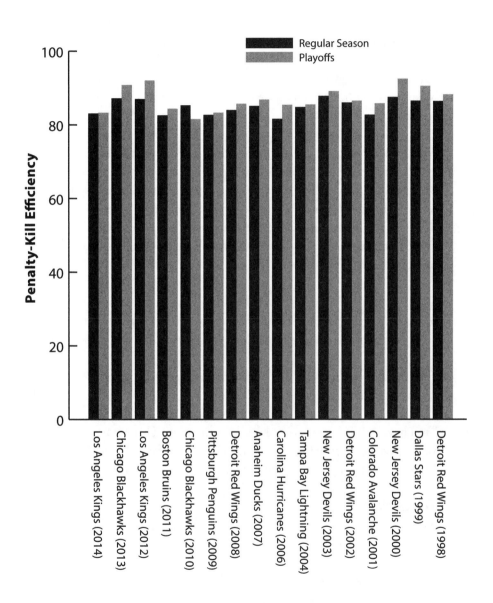

Attempting to block shots to the net? Are they allowing the power play to have an open offensive option while double-teaming another?

The penalty kill is reactionary and situational; it essentially works at two speeds, which are "passive" and "aggressive."

"I prefer to be aggressive. Generally it works better," said former NHLer Mike Johnson, "rather than have them complete pass after pass and gain confidence."

As a team fires the puck around the horn, the PK might sit back and hope for a turnover. The moment there's a vulnerability—an errant pass, a funky rebound, a player without a clear passing outlet—watch how quickly the killers transition to a pressure defense, trying to get the offensive players to run around the zone and give up the puck. Once that pressure starts, it doesn't stop until the puck is cleared—even if it means chasing the puck a bit.

There's also containment around the crease when the puck is sent beneath the goal line. Most teams will collapse into a tight trapezoid around their goalie, attempting to take away passes and second shots.

That means battles in front of the crease, leading to some split-second decision-making from the defense.

"You have a split second to make a determination. This is part of the vast experience that helps defensemen. Do I take away his stick? Do I move him? Do I just hang around and wait for a rebound?" said Ward.

The Goalie
The first thing to watch for is his positioning on the penalty kill compared to where he plays at even strength.

"The penalty kill is the one situation where you'll see, almost to a man, goalies get deeper in their crease. Even the guys who claim to be more aggressive. The power play gives teams the option of lateral passes. If you're too aggressive, you're not going to be able to handle those lateral

» THREE TYPES OF POWER PLAYS

Every team is going to tailor its power play to its personnel. OK, at least in theory—in reality, a coach is going to try to retrofit his particular special teams dogma onto whatever personnel is on the roster, logic be damned.

Here are three different options for the setup of the power play. Keep in mind that in every setup, ideally there will be a left-handed shot on the right boards and vice versa, in order to confuse the defense into guessing shoot or pass.

Spread Power Play: Sometimes also called a split power play, this is your typical setup for the man advantage. Two defensemen man the points; two forwards on the half-boards; one forward in front of the net for a screen. The players spread out through the offensive zone, with most of the setup coming from the point men.

Overload Power Play: While the name conjures visions of smoke and bolts flying around as the offensive machine breaks, it actually describes an overload of players to the strong side of the ice. The player on the half-boards and strong-side point man are the quarterbacks of the power play; in the latter's case, the option to shoot or pass should be just as viable and dangerous for the penalty-killers.

The 1-3-1: This system is preached by power-play guru Adam Oates, and is the system that kickstarted Alex Ovechkin's offense. It's high risk, high reward, as the scheme is designed to allow for blistering one-timers and good puck pursuit down low on rebounds. But it's a variation of the "umbrella" power play in the sense that there's frequently only one defenseman back orchestrating the mayhem. Again, it comes down to personnel—a team has to have a mobile defenseman with great reach and instincts playing the point. One moment spent flat-footed, and that penalty-killer is scoring a shorty.

passes," said Kevin Woodley of *INGOAL* magazine. "It becomes more about shorter, quicker movements to track those passes and to give yourself a chance to make shorter, quicker saves."

Goalies sit in on penalty-kill meetings to learn what the penalty-killers plan on taking away from the other team. If they, say, overcommit on

Ovechkin to defend his one-timer, then the goalie knows he's going to have to be aware of other scoring options potentially having more space.

To that end, there's much more "just stop the puck" on the PK.

"Guys are going to get more clean looks," said Woodley. "So goalies need to have shorter movements in their crease, but also have to know to be more reactive in their saves. If they just get over to a space and try to close their holes, they have to know that shooters have the time and space on a power play to find the corners of the net that are exposed. You can't just drop and block anymore."

The Clear

Clearing the puck isn't as simple as just attempting to send it 200 feet the other way. Watch where the clear is sent—along the boards or the middle of the ice. Watch how the rest of the killers react to the clear—headed to the bench or pursuing the puck for a shorthanded chance.

And, of course, watch as the defenders do their best not to send that biscuit into the stands for a regrettable delay-of-game penalty.

(Seriously, what a hackneyed rule; yes, there are legitimate applications in which a team should be penalized for delaying the game, but there's no discretion in the way the rule is enforced. I once saw Matt Cooke shoot the puck from one end of the ice over the glass at the other end, earning a delay-of-game penalty; is there, like, *any* chance that's what he was going for there?)

The power play–penalty kill disparity is such that I sometimes wish my team could just decline the penalty and play 5-on-5, depending on how they've been rolling (or not rolling) on the man advantage. That's because special teams can determine who wins, who loses, who wins the Art Ross, who fails to get a bigger contract, who has fun, and who successfully prevents others from having fun.

"My favorite thing was pissing off the stars. It was brilliant," said former NHLer Mike Johnson. "It's fun when you can tell they were rattled."

CHAPTER 6

WEAPONS OF CHOICE

It's the story of a boy and his stick.

In 2009, Mike Green of the Washington Capitals had a season for the ages. He scored 31 goals, including an eight-game goal streak that set an NHL record for defensemen. The Hockey Hall of Fame called to ask if it could have the stick that Green used during that streak, no doubt to place it in a warehouse next to the Stovepipe Cup, Jacques Plante's teeth, and the Ark of the Covenant.

Green said no.

He said no because it was from his last 15-stick batch of Easton Stealth CNTs (aka "carbon nanotubes"). He scored every goal in that streak with that stick, and every goal of his season with that stick model. But Easton discontinued the model, so he was using his final twigs. Green thought about sending his gloves instead.

Eventually he decided to earmark that stick for the Hall of Fame. "It's better that it goes to the Hall of Fame than in my garage and I lose it, so I sent it off," he said.

And then, as you might have expected: Green broke his last stick in the batch during Game 1 of the Capitals' series against the Pittsburgh Penguins.

D'oh.

He switched to a heavier stick. After struggling with it, he told reporters, "I felt like I was stick-handling for the first time again."

But he did have one of his old sticks left: sitting in the Capitals' offices, waiting to be shipped to the Hall of Fame. A team employee found it, packed it in a car, and drove four hours to Pittsburgh before Green's next game.

Green refused to use it. Perhaps he felt—like so many fictional heroes throughout history—that the magic wasn't in his weapon of choice, but was inside him all along.

Or perhaps he felt the stupid lumber was going to snap eventually, and then neither he nor the Hall of Fame would have his supernatural, Roy Hobbesian Wonderboy stick.

And that, friends, is how seriously hockey players take their gear.

STICKY HISTORY

The evolution of hockey sticks is a bit like the evolution of hockey itself, going from rigid with no character to flexible and unique to, ultimately, overthought and mechanical.

The first sticks were made of solid ash or birch. They were heavy and had blades as flat as the top of Frankenstein's head, which frequently led to play just as ugly. It wasn't until the 1940s that companies began churning out laminate sticks, and fiberglass coating for those sticks wasn't prevalent until the 1960s. Twenty years later saw the arrival of aluminum sticks, which didn't really catch on until Wayne Gretzky began using one in 1990. (Wooden stick manufacturers considered asking the NHL to ban aluminum, before realizing no one tells the Great One what to do.)

Carbon fiber sticks were the next evolution, a mash-up of wooden sticks' flexibility and aluminum sticks' durability. Then came the last evolution, composite sticks, which are like a stew of different materials (including titanium) boiled up into a lightweight, flexible stick that still snaps every time your team needs a big shot from the point on the power play, like they're evil and sentient.

The blade of the stick evolved slowly. Cy Denneny, a Hall of Fame player for the original Ottawa Senators, is credited with creating the first curved "banana blade" in 1927, using hot water to warp the blade. It gave Denneny a powerful new option for his shots: the long-range slap shot. But his peers were freaked out by the way the blade made stick-handling and backhand shots more difficult, and ignored this heresy.

The banana blade finally hit it big in the 1960s thanks to its adoption by Bobby Hull and Stan Mikita of the Chicago Blackhawks. Their shots would flutter unpredictably at goalies. Others soon adopted the banana blade.

(Perhaps they found it a-peeling. I'll see myself out, thanks…)

That was until 1970, when the NHL mandated that blade size be set at a half-inch, ending the reign of the banana blade. Today, the blade curve is restricted to three-fourths of an inch.

It all depended on how you curve your enthusiasm.

CHOOSE YOUR WEAPON

Hockey players find what works best for them somewhere between the end of their physical maturation and the end of their parents just buying whatever lumber is available in the bargain bucket at the gear store. At that point, players start to establish what kind of flex, size, and curve with which they can most excel. Some will use a stick that's heavier than they're "supposed" to use.

Q: How is illegal gear policed by the NHL?

A: For goalies, nearly every piece of gear is under scrutiny, because the NHL wants to make sure that the guys stopping the pucks don't have an unfair advantage over the guys firing them.

Kay Whitmore was a goaltender in the NHL from 1989 to 2001. (And a former member of the Hartford Whalers. Remember the Whale!) After his playing days, he joined the NHL as its goaltending supervisor. That meant having huge influence over the restrictions and rules the league wanted to place on its netminders. It also meant having to sign off on each goalie's gear every season.

Literally. Every vital piece of goalie gear worn in the NHL has a "K" and a squiggle next to it—Whitmore's initials, inked by hand after he inspects the gear in the NHL's offices in Toronto.

If a player wears gear that doesn't carry his signature, and is caught, it's a two-game suspension, a $25,000 fine for his team, and a $1,000 fine for his equipment manager.

Does that mean the gear can't be messed with after Whitmore has signed off on it? Of course not. But the NHL can administer random,

Some will use lighter sticks, much like how I roll a 10-pound ball at the bowling alley due to my abnormally small hands and desire to bounce it down the lane. (That they're all painted hot pink is my cross to bear.)

Can any player use any stick and still be effective? There are actually two schools of thought on that, and those would be the old school and the new school. An NHL alumnus who played during a time before every stick was tailor-made could probably stick-handle a puck using a Wiffle ball bat. A modern player going from one stick to another is like a surgeon going from a laser scalpel to a hacksaw.

Is it like a batter's relationship with his bat? Certainly, in the sense that a player finds a comfort zone and works with a manufacturer to produce unannounced inspections at any time before, during, or after a game. Which is great, in theory, although this kind of punishment is as rare as Halley's Comet.

Skaters' gear is much less scrutinized, but there are inspections by the league (although the NHL bylaws don't specify any particular penalties).

One piece of gear that is under scrutiny? The stick.

No stick in the NHL shall exceed 63 inches in length from the heel to the end of the shaft, nor more than 12 ½ inches from the heel to the end of the blade. (There is an exception for players who are 6-foot-6 or taller; thanks, Chara.) The blade cannot be less than two inches nor more than three inches wide between the heel and ½ inch in from the midpoint of the tip of the blade.

One team can ask for a stick measurement of an opponent's twig during the game. If it's illegal, the offending player is given a two-minute minor penalty and a fine of $200. Yes, *$200*. The amount of money Evgeni Malkin uses as drink coasters at one of his houses.

If the stick measurement doesn't turn up an illegal stick, the team that inquired about it gets a bench minor penalty and a fine of—wait for it—$100! Less than most tickets to that night's game!

gear to those specs. Is it like a golfer's relationship with his clubs? Yes, in that different weights and "blades" produce different results.

Like any sport whose gear is available wholesale, NHL players frequently have their names placed on sticks in order to better market them. And yet there are some sticks that are endorsed by players who literally have nothing to do with the actual sticks they use. It's like Wolfgang Puck endorsing a pizza he's never made.

But endorsements are big business. Depending on the market, even a third-liner can pull in thousands of dollars by using a company's stick—usually a combination of cold hard cash and other gear from the company.

There are a few essential factors in choosing a stick:

Shape and Size

These are the basics: the shape of the shaft, which can be squared off or rounded; along with the size of the stick, with NHL regulations stating that stick shafts can be a maximum of 63 inches (unless you're a man/mountain like Zdeno Chara and get an exception to use a 65-inch shaft).

While stick size will usually correlate with a player's size, it always comes back to personal preference. A small player like defenseman Mike Weaver used a stick that would have been considered too long for him, but he wielded it well in poke-checking the puck away from foes. Forward David Perron used a shorter stick than one would expect in order to better stick-handle in tight spaces.

Flex

Every stick has a flex number in its name, and that number represents the amount of force in pounds that's required to bend the shaft of the stick exactly one inch, using the bottom hand to apply pressure to the middle of the stick. So an 85 would be a stick that required 85 pounds of force for it to flex an inch.

The flex number is typically determined by a player's size. A smaller player likely wants a smaller number because he has less body weight leaning on the stick into a shot. Daniel Briere, 5-foot-9 and around 175 pounds soaking wet, would start the season with a 90 and then drop all the way down to a 75.

A larger player, like a 6-foot-3 defenseman, needs a higher "flex point" because they apply so much weight on the stick. Imagine someone like Chara with a lower flex point—it would be like watching him play with a swimming pool noodle. Which, given the visual that's all in our heads at the moment, would be hilarious.

The Blade

The curve dictates two things: where the puck "lies" as a player controls it, and where and how the puck comes off the stick.

"You give a guy a different curve, and they won't even be able to shoot the puck," said former NHL forward Mike Johnson.

The "heel curve" generates at the heel of the stick, turning out sideways. The puck is shot from the heel. They're generally better for slap shots and to lean on. The "toe curve" is straighter and kicks in at the middle of the blade to the end. It's better for wrist shots and handling pucks at a distance. But placing that perfect saucer pass is a bit more difficult with the toe curve than the heel.

Then there are "straight curves" like the one with which Sidney Crosby plays. They allow players to handle the puck on their backhand better—Sid's backhand shots could hit a bull's-eye through a pinhole—and are better for faceoffs and to receive passes, even if they aren't ideal for taking booming shots since there's no pocket for the puck to fly off from.

The blade is where you find the most customization for players, which is an odd concept in the NHL. "In a sport where the uniforms are uniform, everyone's stick is different," said Johnson.

That means players take their sticks and snip and cut and burn and warp and whittle like they're Ron Swanson making a chair for Leslie Knope. But they also work closely with manufacturers to create custom blades to their own specifications.

Ryan O'Reilly plays with one that has a severe curve to the toe, passing from the heel or center and using the rest of the blade for wrap-around goals. Mike Cammalleri played with what hockey scribe Justin Bourne called a "dual lie" blade, as a flaw in a batch of sticks gave him two different lies for the puck on his blade. He liked it so much he asked that Easton create more, and soon they were selling "dual lie" sticks in retail.

Then there's Phil Kessel, one of the NHL's most lethal scorers who also has one of the lowest flex-point sticks in the league (somewhere between 65 and 75). As a result, his stick has a low kickpoint that allows him to shoot in stride, using his body weight to whip the puck accurately past the netminder. It's not the strongest stick for puck battles, but it's perfect for a shooter of Phil the Thrill's proportions.

THE LIDS

When Craig MacTavish retired in 1997, he was the last NHL player who was grandfathered into the league's mandatory helmet rule. He skated without a lid for years. His justification: "It was just a comfort thing for me."

Today's players will no doubt sacrifice the cool wind blowing through their mops for the protection against a Shea Weber slap shot braining them like a medieval mace.

Modern hockey helmets are filled with foam cushions, usually either expanded polypropylene (EPP) or dual-density vinyl nitrile (VN). The former is the one used in bike helmets and car bumpers and is rather rigid; the latter has more give and, hence, offers a slightly tighter fit.

Like other hockey gear, the objective with a helmet is to absorb and spread impact. The first line of defense is the shell around the foam, typically made of bonded polycarbonate. Then comes the foam, which absorbs the shock while protecting the head.

About that protection: helmets save players from things like skull fractures and may lessen the effects of direct blows to the head, but they're not some magic force field that prevents concussions. "They will not prevent the angular movements of the head and brain relative to the rest of the body that are responsible for many of the concussions in hockey," said Jonathan Weatherdon of the NHLPA to Fox Sports in 2014.

Oh, but that hasn't stopped companies from trying to elbow into the concussion-prevention market. Bauer was forced to stop advertising that its helmets could prevent brain injuries in 2014 because the science wasn't there to support it. A special concussion-prevention helmet designed by Mark Messier hasn't exactly caught on with players.

The NHL has a few rules for helmets. If a skater loses one during the game, he can continue to play on. But if he returns to the bench on a change, he has to return to the ice with a lid on. Contrast that with the rule about a goalie's mask, which states that play is stopped if he loses it unless the opposing team has the puck and has a scoring chance. But even then we see goalies coddled around the NHL, earning an instant whistle when they lose their masks.

Beginning in 2013, helmet visors became mandatory in the NHL, with a few dozen players who didn't want one grandfathered.

Here's where the modern-day MacTavishes are. I've spoken to a number of players since that rule was passed who disagreed with it. Some because they generally found visors limited their peripheral vision and were distracting—these were some of your more old-school guys who didn't wear them coming up through juniors, as every player does today. Some simply loathed the NHL telling them what kind of safety gear was best for them.

(While we won't get into the general political leanings of NHL players, let's just say this libertarian streak isn't confined to equipment issues.)

THE SWEATERS

There are many colloquial debates in life that are governed by cultural geographic norms. As a native of New Jersey, one of the staples of the Wyshynski family breakfasts was a circular disc of meat called Taylor Ham, so named for John Taylor of Trenton, who first served the greasy little circles of heaven. Yet there are a good number of people—let's call them "wrong"—who instead refer to it as "Pork Roll."

While this is a widely accepted moniker, it also conjures images of sweaty bellies flopping over too-tight swimsuits at Seaside Heights. Appetizing!

In hockey, there are two of these debates regarding nomenclature. *Dressing room* vs. *locker room* is one battlefront, as some argue there are no lockers per se in a hockey dressing room, while others say that the existence of lockers is not a necessity because every team's dressing room is really a locker room. I tend to use the latter, because *dressing room* sounds like I'm trying on cargo shorts at Target, the official uniform of dads everywhere.

The other debate? *Sweater* vs. *jersey*.

This one seemed like a straight-up Canada vs. U.S. throwdown, as Americans tend to use the word *jerseys* and Canadians claim *sweaters*. Yet the Ottawa Senators, in their 20th anniversary season, called their new duds a "heritage jersey." Then Prime Minster Stephen Harper, a major hockey fan, declared that they were actually "jerseys" as well, sparking what we can only imagine was widespread speculation about his impeachment.

The *Ottawa Citizen* found that 70 percent of its readership favored *jerseys* over *sweaters*. Yet when it reached out to Roch Carrier, author of the enduring Canadian children's classic *The Hockey Sweater*, he responded: "A jersey, I understood, was some stuff to do dresses for ladies. That was the ladies' business. Mine was to rush to the skating rink in my hockey sweater..."

So there you go, folks: *sweaters* is the choice for authors with awkward misogynist leanings.

They're called sweaters because it harkens back to the earliest days of pro hockey when that's actually what the players wore: heavy wool sweaters. Gradually they took on the look of what we see today in the Original Six's jerseys: color schemes, numbering, and the like.

Q: Why does the home team wear the colored jersey?

A: The tradition of teams wearing different colored jerseys dates back to 1920, when the Seattle Metropolitans and the Ottawa Senators battled for the Stanley Cup. Seattle's jerseys were red, green, and white; Ottawa's were red, black, and white. Since the uniforms were seen to be too similar in hues, the Senators opted to wear white jerseys.

The home-and-away-jersey contrast wasn't mandated until 1950, and it was due to the advent of newsreel footage of games: the NHL wanted to make sure theatergoers could tell the difference between the Canadiens and the Maple Leafs, besides the obvious tell, which was the Canadiens winning.

At first, the home team wore the colored jersey. It wasn't until the 1970s when the venerable "Hockey Night in Canada" asked the league to mandate home teams wear white in order to spotlight the visiting team's colors.

Then, in 2004, the NHL opted to have the home team wear dark jerseys again. Was it a harken back to days of yore? Of course not! It was so they could sell fans who already owned the white jerseys those road jerseys and, more importantly, those spiffy new revenue-generating third jerseys.

But here's the thing: for centuries, the good guys have generally worn the light colors. The bad guys are the ones who dress in black. One is pure and virtuous; the other is a marauding army of thugs. The NHL is ignoring basic Joseph Campbellesque hero narratives for the sake of pushing the Buffalo Sabres' 10th third jersey in 11 seasons!

So hopefully, one day, they flip back to white jerseys at home.

Except for you, Chicago Blackhawks and Montreal Canadiens. You just keep on wearing dark jerseys to perfection wherever you'd like. Home games. Weddings. As pajamas. Always.

But as time went on, and the players sweated into their sweaters…
well, let's just say the material wasn't exactly competition friendly. In
the sense that it felt like they were skating with an adult yak attached to
them because the wool was so absorbent.

Fast-forward to the 1960s, and we begin to see a more lightweight
material being incorporated into the jerseys: Durene Knit, which was
a nylon-cotton blend that didn't retain nearly as much water. In the
1980s, there was an upgrade to Air-Knit, which breathed a bit better
with a more open weave—look at any jersey beginning around 1985,
and you'll see the tiny holes dotting the Air-Knit material.

Reebok then changed the game after the 2005 lockout with its "RBK
EDGE" material, using 4Way Stretch Pique material to create jerseys
that it claimed would dramatically reduce moisture retention. After a
bumpy start with some teams refusing to wear them, the material was
lauded for keeping the jerseys lighter. (If not more aesthetically pleasing,
with that awful piping.)

Outside of water retention, can a jersey make a player faster? Reebok
sold it this way:

"After extensive testing with experts at MIT (Massachusetts Institute
of Technology), wind tunnel results revealed the new RBK EDGE
uniform generated 9% less drag than the current uniform. These results
were dramatically better than those from aerodynamic tests MIT had
done for other sports. Improvements from tests on other sports resulted
in only a 2-3% increase, at best, over current systems."

So, uh, it sorta works?

The NHL, to the surprise of no one, doesn't tolerate any form of
personalization when it comes to jerseys. Any alteration to the jersey
that's not approved by the league—oversized jerseys, commemorative
patches, anything—can result in a player not being permitted to
participate in a game. Also, each team "shall wear distinctive and

contrasting uniforms for their home and road games, no parts of which shall be interchangeable except the pants."

The NHL: Home of the Interchangeable Pants. How is that not the slogan?

BLADES OF STEEL

The $1,000 hockey skates.

By the time you read this, we might already be there. As of 2015, the high-end skates worn by NHL players typically retailed for around $800, more than double what the low-end weekend-warrior models retail for.

Imagine being able to communicate with someone from the 1920s—perhaps through a mailbox at a lake house, like Keanu—and telling them this, as they look down at the work boot with a steel blade screwed to the bottom of it that they call a "skate." It wasn't until years later that Canadian skate manufacturer Graf helped create the ski-boot design we're familiar with today.

So is this a matter of buying a flashy sports car when that ugly sedan has the same power under the hood? No, actually you're paying for quality in grabbing what the pros wear. The four essential aspects of an NHL player's skate are fit, protection, weight, and durability.

The fit for these high-end skates is great and only gets greater considering how their quarter package holds up to baking (aka heat molding) for a tighter fit. That stiffer quarter package allows not only for a better stride but a better fit.

The protection comes from space-age materials like Kevlar, Teflon, and carbon fiber to protect the foot from the puck. It's the most glaring difference between models by price, as you can see the thick outer casing around the boot.

EQUIPMENT TIMELINE FOR GOALIES

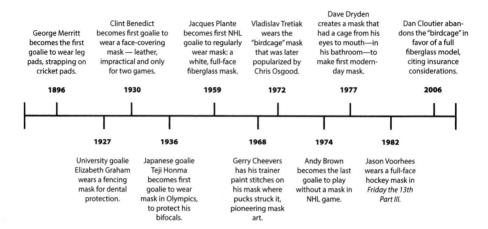

George Merritt becomes the first goalie to wear leg pads, strapping on cricket pads. — 1896

Clint Benedict becomes first goalie to wear a face-covering mask — leather, impractical and only for two games. — 1930

Jacques Plante becomes first NHL goalie to regularly wear mask: a white, full-face fiberglass mask. — 1959

Vladislav Tretiak wears the "birdcage" mask that was later popularized by Chris Osgood. — 1972

Dave Dryden creates a mask that had a cage from his eyes to mouth—in his bathroom—to make first modern-day mask. — 1977

Dan Cloutier abandons the "birdcage" in favor of a full fiberglass model, citing insurance considerations. — 2006

1927 — University goalie Elizabeth Graham wears a fencing mask for dental protection.

1936 — Japanese goalie Teji Honma becomes first goalie to wear mask in Olympics, to protect his bifocals.

1968 — Gerry Cheevers has his trainer paint stitches on his mask where pucks struck it, pioneering mask art.

1974 — Andy Brown becomes the last goalie to play without a mask in NHL game.

1982 — Jason Voorhees wears a full-face hockey mask in *Friday the 13th Part III*.

(Considering how many shots players attempt to block, and how preposterously hard shots in the NHL are, you'd think additional skate guard protection would be mandatory, but it's a piece of equipment that isn't mandated by the NHL.)

But with that protection comes concern about bulkiness, and that's why a lightweight skate that still provides the other factors is essential for NHL players.

The average skate weighs around 1.7 pounds. Around 2006, Bauer, the primary skate producer for the NHL, began swapping out leather for CURV, a composite material that produced a stiffer, lighter skate. But further protection would mean heavier skates, and that's not a swap the players are willing to make.

EQUIPMENT TIMELINE FOR SKATERS

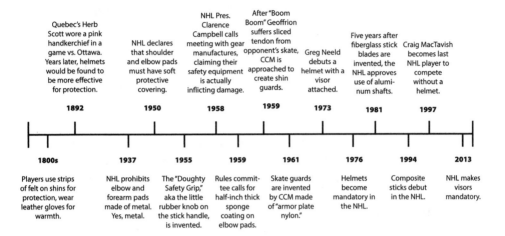

Quebec's Herb Scott wore a pink handkerchief in a game vs. Ottawa. Years later, helmets would be found to be more effective for protection.
1892

NHL declares that shoulder and elbow pads must have soft protective covering.
1950

NHL Pres. Clarence Campbell calls meeting with gear manufactures, claiming their safety equipment is actually inflicting damage.
1958

After "Boom Boom" Geoffrion suffers sliced tendon from opponent's skate, CCM is approached to create shin guards.
1959

Greg Neeld debuts a helmet with a visor attached.
1973

Five years after fiberglass stick blades are invented, the NHL approves use of aluminum shafts.
1981

Craig MacTavish becomes last NHL player to compete without a helmet.
1997

1800s
Players use strips of felt on shins for protection, wear leather gloves for warmth.

1937
NHL prohibits elbow and forearm pads made of metal. Yes, metal.

1955
The "Doughty Safety Grip," aka the little rubber knob on the stick handle, is invented.

1959
Rules committee calls for half-inch thick sponge coating on elbow pads.

1961
Skate guards are invented by CCM made of "armor plate nylon."

1976
Helmets become mandatory in the NHL.

1994
Composite sticks debut in the NHL.

2013
NHL makes visors mandatory.

Then there's durability. An average NHL player goes through about half a dozen pairs of skates in an 82-game season. Some, like Matt Duchene and Steven Stamkos, prefer to keep that number around two.

The biggest issue for durability is the steel. NHL equipment managers are like a one-man NASCAR pit crew when a player "blows a tire," needing to get a skate repaired and ready for action in about four minutes.

That's been revolutionized recently with Bauer's Lightspeed Edge trigger system, which doesn't require the blade be unbolted from the skate. Instead, it's like a disposable razor (although slightly less expensive than any razor with "quattro" in the title) in that it can be swapped out in seconds. Look behind the equipment person on the bench; you might see pockets filled with replacement steel.

Do players swap out skates like they swap out sticks? Not usually, but occasionally you hear about dramatic improvements for players who change their wheels. Bo Horvat, back when he played in junior hockey, had 16 points in 27 games, flipped his skates for a more lightweight model, and then went on a 68-in-61 tear. It happens.

Mostly, players go with the familiar and the comfortable, and then get neurotic about it. Sidney Crosby, for example, gets his skates sharpened *every time* he hits the ice. Which sounds extravagant, but hey, it works.

But Sid's just like every other NHL player: a stickler for his gear, and believing it has to be just right in order to excel. Frequently, that means players will do whatever it takes to keep the gear that works for them.

JR Boucicaut runs Mod Squad Hockey, a hockey gear community on the web. He's worked for several NHL teams as well, and has seen all types of idiosyncrasies among players.

"Brian Leetch's gear was an absolute shit show," he said. "His skates were cross-stitched, little squares all over the place, keeping them together as best he could before having to swap them out."

And then there were Leetch's gloves.

"When he started in 1989, they were red-white-and-blue Easton gloves that he wore for years," said Boucicaut. "Then he broke in another pair some years later in practice, wore those through his trade to the Toronto Maple Leafs, where the red was painted out of it. Then he was traded to Boston, and he was screwed, so he had to get new gloves in 2006.

"But in his entire Hall of Fame career, he had three pairs of gloves."

That's three pairs of gloves for 1,300 games.

That's dedication. Or psychosis. One of the two.

CHAPTER 7

GOALIES (AKA KILLJOYS)

"There is no position in sport as noble as goaltending."
—Vladislav Tretiak, goaltender

"The only job worse is a javelin catcher at a track-and-field meet."
—Lorne "Gump" Worsley, goaltender

Goaltenders are, essentially, the sadomasochists of sports.

They're tasked with nothing short of depriving joy. From fans. From offensive players. From television executives who desperately want more than three goals per game from which to pluck a highlight. They're the Debbie Downers of hockey. Every time a puck flies into their gloves, a sad trombone should play.

But while giving frustration to one team a goalie gives elation to another, provided they excel at this truly deranged profession.

Your job is to stand there while frozen rubber discs are fired at your body. It's like facing a firing squad, except your punishment continues for upwards of 60 minutes. If you don't stop one, you get the blame. Every single person in front of you, from the left defenseman to the cotton candy vendor, can fail to do their job, and it'll be *your fault*. "That's a goal he'll want back!" they'll say, as if there's any other kind.

Yet through all the pain, all the blame, all the stress, and all the strain, goalies are truly the last line of defense; as such, they can be given credit for stealing victories and carrying teams and all the other over-praising that comes from being the one individual who can make or break a game. They're like NFL quarterbacks, minus the college stud looks.

Well, save for Henrik Lundqvist.

Speaking of saves: you've seen goalies make a hundred of them in a week. What you might not have seen are the reasons behind each save—the decisions, the positioning, the blind trust placed in teammates' competence—that help determine which group's joy the netminder will kill in that instance.

It begins with style.

BETWEEN THE POLES POSITION

In Game 3 of the 2011 Stanley Cup Final—the most compelling championship round I've seen as a hockey fan, for what it's worth— Tim Thomas of the Boston Bruins gave up a goal to Maxime Lapierre in the third period that ended up being the difference in a 1–0 shutout by Roberto Luongo of the Vancouver Canucks.

After the game, Luongo was asked about that goal, and the rest is goalie smack-talk history.

"It's not hard if you're playing in the paint," said Luongo. "It's an easy save for me, but if you're wandering out and aggressive like he does, that's going to happen."

Luongo would go on to say he had been "pumping Thomas' tires since the series started" and that he hadn't "heard one nice thing he had to say about me." Thomas infamously volleyed back with "I guess I didn't realize it was my job to pump his tires," a burn that continues to smolder to this day.

The point of Luongo's comment was that, essentially, every goalie thinks his brand of kung fu is the strongest.

Luongo is a classic butterfly-style goaltender: a wide stance, his feet falling in behind him when he drops down, as his five-hole closes up with his knees. The butterfly style wasn't actually en vogue until Thomas was in his early twenties; he was a hybrid goalie, taking some of that technique but ultimately relying more on instinct, which is why he used to flop around the crease like someone's goldfish after the house cat knocked over the bowl.

There are also different types of styles within the butterfly. There's the narrow butterfly, where a goalie's feet fall behind him. Those goalies tend to close their five-hole with their knees. And there are wider butterflies, where a goalie is spread farther out and you see a wall of pads when he goes down.

It comes down to this for goalies: what are you taking away from a shooter, and what are you leaving behind?

Henrik Lundqvist of the New York Rangers plays "deep in his net," closer to the goal line. He wants that three or four extra feet to give himself time to react. The farther back one plays, the shorter the distance one needs to travel to make a save or recover after making one on every lateral play.

Let's say a defenseman on the left point makes a pass to the right point. If Lundqvist has his left skate on his left post, he basically just rotates his torso to square to the shooter. His skate maybe moves two feet, as he goes left post to right post. It allows him to move quicker and get set more quickly. It's a remarkable difference from a goalie who plays higher up and needs to stride to face the shooter.

Yes, Lundqvist's style gives the shooter more to look at, but Lundqvist luckily has a secret weapon, which is locking eyes with the shooter and having them get lost in their dreaminess. (Just kidding. We think.)

Q: We've all seen players take runs at goalies. How do goalies fight back?

A: Funny thing about a goalie stick to a gentleman's undercarriage: it'll tend to clear traffic from in front of the crease.

Watching the battle between a goalie and players attempting to screen him is one of the best "game within a games" you're going to see. While in the past it was netminders like Ron Hextall and Billy Smith chopping down defensemen like lumberjacks clearing a forest, today's goalies are a bit less violent but just as inherently aggressive.

Goalies will typically use their gloves to push a skater farther away from them if the screen is established in their crease. This is a legal play: a goalie has a right to initiate contact to establish position.

The attacking player needs to vacate that position or the referee can call a minor penalty. Actual NHL rulebook justification: "This player runs the risk of 'bad things' happening."

Bad things!

Basically, goalies are coddled by that rulebook and use it to their advantage. Anything they do—a little whack to the back of the knee, for example—could be explained away by "establishing position." Even the plays involving excessive force, like the aforementioned club to the nether-regions, can result in the goalie *and* the guy he whacked getting coincidental penalties.

The biggest crutches a goalie has from the referees are the vague goaltender interference rules. Any contact with a goalie that prevents him from making a save will undoubtedly be considered goalie interference, resulting in a disallowed goal and/or a penalty on the player. Even plays that don't result in contact can be whistled: if an attacking player skates through the crease, in front of a goalie's eyes, as the puck crossed the line, the goal is disallowed.

Put it this way: the NHL rulebook's table on goalie interference has 32 different scenarios listed.

And the less said about a goalie drawing penalties by flopping around like a marionette that just had its strings cut, the better. NFL quarterbacks wish they were that coddled by officials.

He's also a freak. Not many goalies have his instincts and reflexes, so not many play as deep in the crease as Lundqvist does. Some play mid-crease; others get very aggressive and challenge the shooters at the top of the crease.

What are the benefits to each position?

The farther out a goalie plays, the more vision and space he's taking away from the shooter. There's less chance a goalie will be beaten cleanly from the outside.

"The farther you're out, the more the angle from the puck to the post, the more of that space you're taking up in that triangle from the cut to the post. In other words, cutting down the angle," said Kevin Woodley of *INGOAL* magazine. "The farther you get out, the more you cut down that angle, just by being in position."

There's also more room for backward motion, which some goalies prefer, gliding back when challenged by the shooter, cutting down the angle. That was the "starting outside-in" style of Martin Brodeur.

A goalie who plays at the top of his crease has a significant distance to travel when faced with a one-timer. Ultimately what's taught by goalie coaches is for goalies who play high to move back toward their post when the puck is being passed around laterally, until he feels he's "center net" in terms of his angle to the shooter. Only then should the goalie come back out and add depth to his positioning.

Brodeur was the greatest goalie of all time based on the numbers. He was a butterfly goalie when he was younger, but when he got to the NHL and worked with Devils goaltending coach Jacques Caron, he decided it wasn't enough to just block the puck. He wanted to be more mobile within his crease.

Not exactly blessed with what you'd call great mobility—Brodeur had the numbers of Patrick Roy and the physique of Patrick the Starfish from *SpongeBob SquarePants*—he worked on what are called T-pushes.

WHERE GOALIES ARE BEATEN

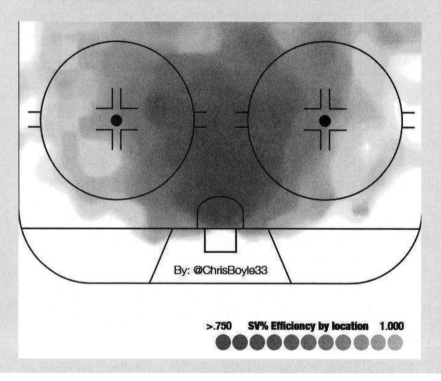

By: @ChrisBoyle33

>.750   SV% Efficiency by location   1.000

Here's how that works: a goalie opens the leg on the side of his body in the direction in which he wants to travel. His skates will be perpendicular. Knees bent, he pushes off with his trailing leg, and how much weight he puts on his front skate will determine how far he'll travel.

It's an old-school method, but Brodeur was an old-school goalie.

"I think the trend of butterfly—stats don't lie, it works," he told *INGOAL* magazine. "So you can't bash that. It's all about percentages. It was successful at one point and so that's how goalie coaches taught the younger guys to play the game. They'll tell you how many percent of the goals in the NHL are scored in certain areas of the net and if you're able to block it at 100 percent, you should be a good goalie.

"But I think it's gotten tougher and tougher just to think about percentages because there is a lot more wide-open shots, a lot more survival out there than there was before the lockout. Your reflex game is more important, your agility, being able to recover from a save and controlling your rebounds are more important now because your defensemen can't do the job they used to be able to do by interfering with players trying to get rebounds. Guys are able now to get the rebounds, so just blocking the shot is going to get tougher on goalies to just rely on that. You're really going to have to control your game, put the puck where you want as far as rebounds are concerned."

And even when a goalie sets up perfectly, there are risks.

"When you don't set your feet, it's way harder to make certain saves. And then when you do, you're so far from the net you can't make another one," said goalie coach Mitch Korn.

So just like goalies take a little bit o'butterfly for their style, they'll also take a little bit of the crease. Many play at a three-quarters' depth, trying to get the best of both worlds: a lot less distance when recovering to make the next save than a guy a foot higher in the crease, but cutting down more of the net than the cardboard shooting target playing off his goal line (again, Lundqvist excluded).

"That's where goalie coaching has evolved," said Woodley. "They look for ways to move around the crease to ensure coverage. That you can get to the next space as quick as you can be. They look for efficiencies in ways to get there. Like on a one-timer, when a goalie slides back toward his post on his knees—at the very least, he's cutting off the bottom of the net. He's taking away that space."

In some ways, it sounds like goaltending is a variation on that old Wayne Gretzky mantra about being where the puck isn't.

"Except that in Gretzky's case, there was a lot more flow and circular movement. Goalies go into the space and fill it as quickly as possible.

Not where the puck isn't, but rather where it should arrive via the angle," Woodley said.

Even if goalies argue about their styles like grandmothers argue over pie ingredients at a county fair, it all comes back to one thing: making the save. And no two are alike, in execution or purpose.

SAVE US!

The first thing to know about goalies is that they're not actually making a play on the puck.

No, they're making a play on the *situation*. Where the shot originates, where the rest of the players are on the ice. Blocking the puck is the ultimate objective, but cutting down the probabilities of it going in—on a first or second or third attempt—is the aim.

What makes goaltending such an insanely paced position is that a goalie sometimes faces several situations in the same sequence. Contrast that with other defensive players in pro sports: a pitcher faces one situation on every pitch; a defensive lineman faces one on every snap. In hockey, the puck can pinball around the offensive zone for 25 seconds, generating five good chances.

During the 2014–15 regular season, there were 43.75 shot attempts per team each game, which includes any that hit the goal, went wide, or were deflected, at even strength or on special teams. Two teams, the Stanley Cup champion Chicago Blackhawks and the New York Islanders, had more than 4,000 shot attempts in 2014–15.

The goalie's decisions change based on the situation. On a penalty kill, a goalie has to make sure his movements laterally are short distances. On a 2-on-1 break, a goalie prays to the hockey gods that his defenseman has the pass covered and aggressively challenges the other shooter; or failing that, attempts to cheat and anticipate the pass.

Then there are some unanticipated situations, like when a puck is tipped. When it happens in front of a goalie, point-blank, there are learned movements he can make to block it—goalies practice tip-drills all the time. When it happens 35 feet away, a goalie has no depth perception as to where the puck is headed. It needs to travel for a while. He can react to the shot leaving a player's stick, but if it's deflected, it's the point of no return after he's committed to his save.

In that sense, goalies are like the protagonist in any video game that involves weaponry. Just as you scroll through your guns and swords to figure out how to get past that three-headed computer-controlled alien warrior from the planet Gleep-Glorp, a goalie has his own arsenal from which to choose.

It's a concept called "save selection." In a split second, a goalie must determine how he will attempt to make a save, what he'll utilize to make it, and how he'll make the next one. Even on a "bad" play, understanding what a goalie is trying to accomplish is the difference between justified criticism and unnecessary blame.

For example, imagine a long shot on goal from just inside the blue line. A goalie could snag it with his glove to earn a faceoff if his team is tired; he could catch it, drop it, and keep it in play; he could block it with his chest, have it fall to the ice, and cover it; he can steer it with his stick or with a kick save to the corner, for his defenseman to gather; or he could attempt to kick it back though the zone, past the oncoming forecheck.

The farther out the shot arrives from, the more a team expects its goalie to be able to control the puck. It becomes less about stopping the shot in that moment and more about strategy.

Think of goaltending like a game of pool: it's not the ball you knock in the pocket, it's how you set up the next two or three shots. Same holds for a goalie: that initial save could be technically flawless, but if it left him out of position for save No. 2 then he's probably got a good view of the puck crossing the goal line.

» CHEATERS!

Goalies cheat.

No, seriously, there's actually a piece of equipment called "the cheater."

It's a panel located next to the thumb on a goalie's catching glove that gives a goalie a wider area of coverage when he flashes his glove up. It originated with goalie Mike Palmateer, who showed up one day at practice with extra material running from the thumb of his glove to the wrist. Within weeks, everyone else was doing it, because goalies are cheaters.

"It protects the thumb from being broken," claimed goaltending analyst Kevin Woodley (although he admitted that some of the "cheaters" were so egregious that it looked like the goalies "could have scooped up salmon out of the river" with the equipment).

The NHL has (allegedly) cracked down on equipment that give goalies an unfair advantage through the years. The goalies and the NHLPA have fought back, claiming safety issues should trump a desire to shrink pads to non-Michelin Man levels.

"I think [NHL goaltending supervisor] Kay Whitmore has done a very good job in balancing the safety of the players with reducing the size of the equipment," said Woodley. "But we have to be really careful with some of this stuff."

Pekka Rinne is one NHL goaltender whose rebound control is his calling card. "As primitive as our advanced stats are for goaltenders, they seem to indicate he has the best rebound control. He catches everything," said Woodley. "When there's a long shot on Pekka, he will actually reach down in front of his pads with his glove and scoop it like a shortstop, whereas with a lot of goaltenders in North America, the instinct is going to be to use your pads for a puck along the ice. It's an easy save—use their stick to move it to the corner, or kick it into the corner. Well, that gives the forwards the advantage, because they can see

Here are some of the other ways goalies are dirty stinkin' cheaters who cheat.

Knee Pads: The easiest, most common way for a goalie to skirt restrictions on pad size. There are these large knee pads that goalies wear that are manufactured in Switzerland and layered on top of each other. The NHL restricts their size to nine inches but permits layering. When a goalie drops, the knee pads help seal up the five-hole, leading to some complaints about goalies "making saves they shouldn't make." It's necessary protection, but there's no question that players use them to cheat.

Boot Strap: Henrik Lundqvist led the way for goalies who loosen the strap that connects their pads to their skates. While most don't like the extra movement when they rotate their pads, some keep it loose so the pad seals to the ice faster, the broad face of it facing the shooter. Some goalies don't even connect the strap altogether, making their pads sit just a tad higher on their legs.

Pushing Off the Post: In the 2014 Olympic Games, Russia cried foul because U.S. goalie Jonathan Quick kicked the goal post off its mooring while making a save. No one noticed it. The Russians later scored a goal that was waved off because of it. Savvy play by a goalie known for this sneaky bit of quasi-legal delay of game, something other goalies practice.

The Flop: Goaltender interference rules being what they are, netminders can draw penalties around their crease and behind the net with relative ease. Which is why it's been a rumored target for expanding video reviews for some time.

where the puck is going and the defensemen have to turn around and go find it and get it.

"What Pekka does is scoop it off the ice for a faceoff. You're not going to win them all, but you have a better opportunity to possess the puck if you have a faceoff. [Defenseman] Shea Weber said there are about six or seven situations each game where he figures Pekka catches the puck where no other goalie does. So that's six or seven fewer times that the defensemen are scrambling to control a rebound out of their own end."

Communication with his defense and an understanding of what offensive attack is ahead of him is essential in scrolling through his save arsenal to choose what works best. A save in a high-scoring area, for example, will hopefully result in a dead puck; a blocking save on a bad angle might keep it in play. Sometimes a big rebound isn't a bad rebound, so long as the puck isn't gift wrapped for the opposition.

The goalie is always thinking about what's in front of him, both on his team and on the opposing team. The most cerebral of them believe that they're the ones controlling play—that they're proactive rather than reactive, in affecting a shooter's approach.

"Ryan Miller likes to dictate," said Woodley. "He's an active goalie, and he can dictate decisions for shooters based on his positioning. Goalies at the NHL level are aware of what's in front of them to the point of knowing if the puck-carrier is a right- or left-hand shot, and if his pass option is a left shot or a right shot. He can see that as far away as center ice as a play starts to develop. The best at that level can process it that quickly."

Take a 2-on-1, for example. Sometimes the play is dictated by what the defenseman does. But just as often, it's the goaltender who can influence a pass by aggressively challenging the shooter. And whether or not that shooter has an easier shot or pass attempt based on whether he's a righty or a lefty can determine how aggressive the goalie is on the odd-man rush.

But in the end, it's all about reducing risk of a mistake. A poke-check with his stick, for example, is pretty much a 50/50 proposition, which is why it typically carries the adjective "desperate." Overplaying the shooter means a more dramatic recovery if he completes the pass.

Which is to say that even the best intentions when selecting a save might not work out.

"Not all five-hole goals are bad goals," says Korn of that area between the thighs. "Say a guy's eight feet away from you. You choose to stay on your feet. He blows it in back of you, through your five-hole. You're not humanly able to get down fast enough. So there's a strategy some guys use where they slide or they drop down, and they take their five-hole away. But now they become vulnerable, left and right. How many times have you heard a coach say he went down early, and the shooter roofed him? Then a few games later, he stays up and gets beat through the five-hole, and the coach says he didn't cover the five-hole. You can't win."

No, you can't if you're a goalie. Make 39 saves, and they'll complain you didn't get the 40th.

No wonder they're all insane.

THE MENTAL GAME

You'll have to forgive NHL goalies if a few of them approach team skates like Allen Iverson used to approach off-day shootarounds.

"I'm biased. I lost an appendix to a slap shot," said Woodley. "It has to be said: most practices are [expletive] useless for goalies. Oh god… that's where you get hurt. Guys in practice get 10 to 20 shots on goal that they won't get but once in a season. Maybe even once in a career— wide-open, just put-your-head-down-and-fire looks. It's nuts.

"And here's the other part of it: what purpose does it serve for the shooters? They come down that wing on 3-on-0 drills, and they blast the puck, always trying to pick a corner. But then we get into a game situation, and if that guy dares to take that shot, missed the net, and the puck goes back the other way, the coach is going nuts on that shooter. So practices are bad for goaltenders, and they put shooters in situations that they never see in a game. It makes *no* sense."

OK, so maybe practice has its flaws. But what about the pregame skate?

One thing I love to do when I arrive at the arena before a game is watch the goalies get into the zone. And by that I mean, enter into some bizarre voodoo trance that would end up with them in a padded room had they performed it in the middle of a busy sidewalk.

Braden Holtby of the Washington Capitals is, for my money, the personification of this creepy goalie tradition. He'll put his goalie stick to his mouth, blade up, and start rotating his head back and forth, eyes wide open. Then he'll slip the blade over his eyes and move back and forth, almost wearing the stick like a blindfold.

The routine continues during the game. During stoppages, you continue to see him dart his eyes around with his mask off. Occasionally, he'll actually squirt his water bottle into the air and track the liquid with his vision, like he's the dog from *Duck Hunt* tracking fowl.

There is a (scientific) method to this madness. John Stevenson is an Alberta-based sports psychologist who helped train Holtby in the ways of visualization. That includes *Kaizen*, a Japanese concept for continuous improvement that Holtby adopted to the point of having two Japanese characters on his mask that represent it.

What Stevenson found was that Holtby had a knack for mimicking other goalies just by watching them. Holtby said that process began when he watched Hall of Famer Patrick Roy as a young fan.

"I haven't seen that in any other goaltender ever. The way [Roy] competed, and not only competed but was able to raise his level once things got hard and once his back was against the wall in order to do something. He needed to step up and be a leader on his team," Holtby told the *Washington Times*. "As a goalie it's not always the easiest thing to be a leader on a team....Whenever you see a guy like that that his teammates look up to, you know his qualities are outstanding, and that's just what I try and model myself after."

Roy was also an acolyte of visualization as a young goalie, thanks in great part to his father, Michel. He taught his son a technique that would stick with him through the years: when he was in bed ready to

Q. Are goalies just destined to be injured more than skaters?

A: During the 2014–15 season, the top 25 goalies in games played averaged 59.88 games. Some worked in tandem, some were given considerable rest during the season, but others were injured during the season, albeit sometimes only for a game or two.

The fact is that goalies are contorting their bodies in ways that lend themselves to groin injuries, sometimes chronically. But it goes beyond overstretching to make a save.

Much like there's nothing natural about a pitcher's arm rotation, leading to more-than-occasional injuries in baseball, a butterfly goalie is putting himself at risk for injuries down the line.

"The human hip was not designed to butterfly. It's not a natural human function, which is why you see so many hip injuries. That hip joint was not designed to internally rotate, and the butterfly is the internal rotations of the hip joint," said Kevin Woodley of *INGOAL* magazine. "If there are any imperfections at the top of the femur, if it's not perfectly round in that socket, it's going to carve out the cartilage in the joint. It needs to be perfectly round."

There have been some iron man goalies such as Martin Brodeur, and there have been some goalies who have been the health equivalent of a wet piece of tissue paper (but enough about Rick DiPietro). But goalie injuries will happen, lest you believe someone going into yoga poses to stop 90-mph frozen rubber discs is somehow impervious to the game's various injury demons.

fall asleep, Patrick would go over in his mind the way his opponent plays the game and picture how he'd react in certain situations. Seeing a shot, responding to the dekes. Sometimes they would score on him; in his mind, Dream Patrick would calmly take the puck out of the net to show his Dream Teammates that he wasn't rattled.

When he would play the game the next day, Roy said there would be no surprises.

Of course, scientific visualization and mental exercises only get you so far. Please keep in mind that goalies like Roy and others are…what's the clinical term…"freakin' bananas," I believe.

Roy used to lay out each piece of his gear in the dressing room, and would only dress himself in a specific order. He would never skate over the blue line or red line—he'd step or leap over them. He would stare at his net, picturing it smaller than it actually was.

Oh, yeah—he also would have conversations with his goal posts, which wasn't at all crazy. An actual conversation Roy had with reporters while playing in Montreal:

"Before the game, you skate halfway toward the blue line, then turn and face your net. Why do you do that?"

"I talk to my goal posts."

"And…do they answer?"

"Sometimes…sometimes they say 'Ping' when they make a save."

Quirky? Sure. Crazy? Maybe a little. Effective? Well, they do call him "Hall of Famer Patrick Roy."

But the key for Roy, or really any goalie, wasn't found in his pregame mind's eye or his in-game superstitions. It was actually found in their postgame experiences, as the good ones let their mistakes eat at them and the great ones learn—in the words of Queen Elsa from *Frozen*—to let it go.

Brian Elliott had a good take on that aspect of job, via *The Power Within*:

"We had a team psychologist who was with Edmonton in the Mark Messier and Wayne Gretzky days. When I was struggling in the AHL, we went out to lunch because I was worrying about things, and I was feeling the pressure of not producing wins in my first year as a pro. He said, 'What can we do about it? Are you worrying about it?' and I said, 'Well, yeah, I'm worrying. This is what I want to do, and I'm not doing it, and I don't know what to do about it.' And he said, 'Well, how about I come over to your place later tonight and we'll sit down and worry together, and we can worry for however long you want. I'll stay up all night and worry with you if you want.' You laugh after that, and that was it. That was his lesson; what is worrying really going to do for you? It's counter-productive. I can worry all night about things, but it's not going to get me anywhere. So you have to let it go, because worrying doesn't do anything for you."

Easier said than done when everything is always your fault. But that pressure is what drives them; that pain is what defines them, and their ability to work through it all is the difference between winning a Vezina and being a sieve.

Hence, goaltenders are, essentially, the sadomasochists of sports.

CHAPTER 8

THE NASTY BITS

How did you become a hockey fan?

My journey is a painful one. Not for me, but for others.

I grew up in New Jersey. My father was an Islanders fan before the Devils relocated from Colorado to the swamps of East Rutherford, and before his son started putting posters of Martin Brodeur on his bedroom walls. He loved watching hockey, but more than that he loved going to the arena to watch hockey. So before I ever picked up a stick, my first exposure to the game was in a seat at the Meadowlands.

A cheap seat. I don't want to say my father got the most affordable tickets in the place, but I'm pretty sure halfway up the stairs to those nosebleeds we actually passed an angel sitting on a cloud playing "Rock & Roll (Part II)" on a harp.

But it was there that my passion for hockey was forged. My dad would take me to the right games: Devils vs. Rangers. Devils vs. Flyers. Devils vs. Islanders. Devils vs. Capitals. Patrick Division blood feuds. Games that featured fights on the ice. Games that featured fights in the stands. It was chaos. It was dangerous. It was a series of deplorable acts that would result in immediate incarceration had they occurred anywhere but an NHL rink.

It was hockey. And I was in love.

I have trouble wrapping my brain around the game I fell in love with and the game I cover today. I talk to newbie hockey fans and it's like my dad trying to explain to me that you used to be able to smoke on an airplane: *How on earth could they allow that to happen, given what we know today about health and safety?*

It's tough to square my appreciation of Scott Stevens taking off Eric Lindros' head in the 2000 Stanley Cup playoffs, and my acknowledgment that such hits directly lead to years of hell from concussion symptoms. It's seemingly fruitless to celebrate goons when they've been legislated out of the NHL, and when the actions of the remaining few are now decried as "bad for the game."

I talk about my dad buying tickets to a game just to see Bob Probert fight a Devil, and it's like a Roman justifying having season tickets to Christians vs. lions.

And yet it's the punchers and the dirty players and the rats that give the game color.

It's their existence that gives hockey its rough edges and its blue-collar aesthetic. It's a sport where some of the greatest athletes in the world exhibit unparalleled skill and make millions, while at the same time being a sport that allows a more marginal talent to punch and hit his way into achieving his dream of being a pro hockey player.

Paul Bissonnette was one such marginal talent.

WHY THEY FIGHT

Paul Bissonnette is better known as "Biz Nasty," an enforcer for the Phoenix Coyotes during his NHL career who gained a cult following for his social media presence.

He was taken in the fourth round of the 2003 NHL Entry Draft. Back then, he wasn't much of a fighter. "I didn't do it growing up. I reached

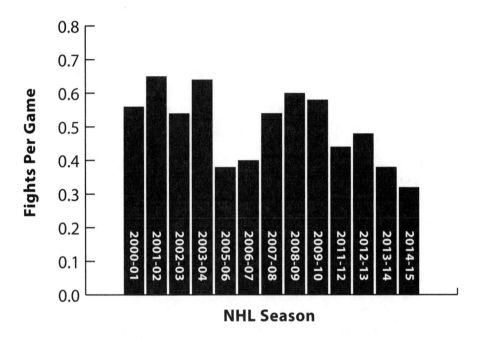

FIGHTS PER GAME IN NHL

a point where I was a D-man, and they switched me to forward, and I was like, 'I gotta add another element to my game.' I was an effective fourth-liner in the American League. But I felt like I was big enough, so why not fight, too?" he said.

Around 2007, his penalty minutes went from double to triple digits: 188 that season, followed by 176 more in the American Hockey League in 2008–09. That's when he got the call from the Pittsburgh Penguins, before being claimed on waivers by the Phoenix Coyotes.

"So there were two years of growing pains. That was when the American League was pretty tough, back when they had a few mutants playing," he said.

Brad May was a more accomplished junior player, but with a similar story. May posted ridiculous numbers in the OHL: 181 points in 160 games. He was a first-round pick of the Buffalo Sabres in 1990. But when he joined the team, he found there was too much competition at his position.

"I was never in a fight. We were all good hockey players, playing junior, playing midget. I had 37 goals in 34 games. When I get to the NHL, every other player that's challenging for that same position had similar numbers. A similar pedigree. But I was not going to be better than them at 19 years old," he said.

So May fought. A lot. As a 20-year-old in 1991–92, he amassed 309 penalty minutes in just 69 games. The next season, it was 242 in 82 games. "I found a niche," he said.

The short answer to "Why do they fight?" is "Because it's their job." The longer answer is that players feel that fighting has a place in the game, both as a deterrent and as a tactic.

"Being a teammate in the NHL, there are a number of reasons you fight. Because you don't like the guy across from you. Because he disrespected the guy next to you. Because no one touches my brother," said May.

Fighters will tell you that the threat of the fight is just as important as actual retribution. "Some teams have small skilled guys. A bigger guy can take advantage of him all night. So why not send someone like me out there for a shift?" said Bissonnette.

It's a time-honored personnel move in the NHL, even today: get a pugilist to "protect" your stars. The Penguins would add muscle to protect Sidney Crosby. The Blackhawks would roll fourth-liners who could avenge Jonathan Toews and Patrick Kane. It dates back to Wayne Gretzky having Dave Semenko and Marty McSorley get his back in the 1980s.

The thinking is that their presence in the game would deter opponents from making a dirty hit on a skill player. And while dirty hits happen every night even with the presence of fighters, players swear by that credo.

"If they take fighting out, and guys aren't worried about answering the bell, I guarantee more people will get hurt from an increase in open-ice body checks. How do I know for a fact? Because I think about it myself all the time as an enforcer," Brandon Prust wrote on The Players' Tribune in 2015. "If I know there's a guy on the other team who might kick my ass at any second, I'm thinking twice about taking a guy's head off going across the middle. Enforcers feel fear, too."

But enforcers also exact revenge. "The Code" is the unwritten rules of the fighting game, passed on through the generations, even when the passing of time makes some of its elements archaic. It lays out a code of honor within a fight—no eye gouging or hair pulling!—but it also dictates how retribution should be delivered to an opponent for taking liberties with your teammate.

"It's all about willingness. You have to be all-in, and I was. And I found that when I fought for my teammates, I was better at it. More emotionally engaged," said Bissonnette.

There have been two instances in recent NHL history where the Code fell apart. The first was in 2004, when Todd Bertuzzi of the Vancouver Canucks punched Steve Moore of the Colorado Avalanche in the back of the head as retribution for a hit Moore put on Bertuzzi's teammate Markus Naslund. The incident, after which Moore was motionless and then stretchered off the ice, ended up leading NBC's *The TODAY Show* the next morning. The aftermath: Moore never played again, Bertuzzi was suspended 20 games, and lawsuits filed by Moore against Bertuzzi and others lingered into 2014 before there was an out-of-court settlement.

The other incident was the attack by Shawn Thornton of the Bruins on Brooks Orpik of the Penguins in 2013, after Orpik delivered a hard but legal hit on Thornton's teammate Loui Eriksson. Thornton tried to fight Orpik, who didn't engage; later in the game, he tripped him to the ice, slammed his head down, and punched him. Orpik left on a stretcher and Thornton was suspended 15 games.

Again, the Code was debated: should Orpik have fought to defuse the situation?

"If you're my teammate, nobody hits you," said May. "As a player? Orpik, who cracks guys all the time with hits, has a responsibility to face Shawn Thornton in that moment."

Said Bissonnette: "I know the pressure from the fans and maybe even some media on Thornton. Orpik hits one of your guys, and your guys are looking at you to get that retribution for your team. I'm not saying Orpik should have fought. But he could have defused the situation."

Why do they fight? Sometimes, it's because someone tells them to, because their team needs a boost. A fight can seemingly spark a team to rally in a game in which they're not emotionally engaged.

There's some evidence that points to a marginal boost—*The Hockey News* took 50 random fights from 2012–13 and found there was an increase from 0.67 shot attempts per minute before a fight to 0.83 per minute after a fight. But much of the praise for it is anecdotal.

That said, it's something many coaches believe to be true, both in how a fight can shift momentum to a team as well as away from another.

"The coaches are always like, 'We're up two. Don't even engage with that guy,'" recalled Bissonnette. "Unless he takes a run at one of your guys."

Why do they fight? Because it's the entertainment industry, and fighting is undoubtedly still a part of the package for a great many fans.

It's relied on in the minor leagues as a gate attraction, especially in non-traditional markets in the U.S. But many of the sideshow aspects of fighting have gone by the wayside in the NHL as the league has cracked down on "staged fights" after faceoffs and at the end of games.

HOW THEY FIGHT

Fighting is as much a skill in hockey as taking a slap shot. It's something honed and practiced and studied by its users.

A fight can happen organically, in the flow of play, as two guys battle. It can be something prearranged, from a previous shift or because the coaches have decided there's going to be a fight and deployed the prerequisite talent. It can be something as simple as one player uttering "You wanna go?" and then we're off to the punches.

The first key to the fight is "the grab." Watch a fight: rarely do you see two fighters engage without tugging on each other's gear in an act of defense.

"The grab's really important. I'm more of a defensive fighter. I like to grab the jersey, keep him away with left, and jab 'em. People think that's kind of soft, but those jabs throw him off and he gets irritated. He'll make a mistake," said Bissonnette. "I would watch YouTube clips of guys. It's nice visually to see how they come in. The grab was important to me. But you need to see if they're going to try and bring you in for a quick shot, twist you, and get another big shot."

One thing lost on many who watch hockey fights is that the hockey fights are happening…on ice. There's a skill in keeping one's leverage and balance during the fight when you're not on terra firma, especially in delivering punches with force.

Said Brent Severyn, a former enforcer in the NHL, on his website: "Once the gloves are off, the pressure, tension, and mental energy explode in a huge release of violence. Your instincts and strategy take over. I fought so often that I could feel my adversary's movement and tell you what hand he was throwing, I didn't have to look. When your punch connects, you feel it in your hands and through your body. I also knew if I was throwing wildly. You sense when you are off-balance or your rhythm is wrong. Being unsettled in a fight usually portends danger. The first rule of the fight club is to never look down. If you do, you are open to a devastating uppercut. Sometimes when I really got tagged I would see a bright starburst in my head, almost like lightning. I thought I was soft and it was a sign of weakness until I interviewed Ultimate Fighting champion Matt Hughes years later and he said he felt the same thing when he was hit hard."

Wrote Prust: "Once the gloves fall off, everything else kind of fades away. You can't hear the fans. You can't hear the ref. It's just silence. That's the easy part. The tough part is the day leading up to the game when you know you're going up against a tough guy. You can't help but think about it all day, and you go through a roller coaster of emotions. It can be almost impossible to think about the actual hockey part of the game. You definitely lose some sleep at nap time.

"This is not a bad thing. I fight my best when I'm well prepared but when I'm also a little nervous. If you go into a fight where you're not worried, you're not going to be as prepared. I watch videos on guys I know I might have to fight just to be ready for the kind of punches they throw and their tendencies. What hand are they coming out with? When do they like to switch hands? Do they like to grab the jersey? I'm only 6-foot, 195 pounds. My margin for error is small. If I don't grapple a guy and get him in close, I might wind up throwing a right and landing three inches short of his face and then get split for seven stitches."

The end of a fight is always an interesting moment. It usually occurs when one player topples onto the other, and if it's the home team guy on top the fans will pop even if his face was a bloody pulp from losing the fight.

Q: How much does fighting add to hockey's concussion problem?

A: The NHL has itself a bit of a contradiction when it comes to player safety: how does the league square establishing draconian rules against contact with an opponent's head on open-ice checks, in the name of preventing concussions, while at the same time giving a winking endorsement to the convention of fighting?

To hear the NHL explain it, a hockey fight involves two willful combatants while, say, a blindside hit isn't something a player will sign off on. But that doesn't change the fact that fights contribute to the league's concussion problem.

Or do they? A study of more than 710 fights in the 2010–11 season by Georgetown University School of Medicine found that the risk of concussion in a fight was much lower for brawling hockey players (0.39 percent) compared to the per-game risk for those who checked one another (nearly 4.5 percent). They cited the lack of velocity on some punches because it was hard for combatants to gain traction on the ice for a fight.

Of course, the counterargument to these findings is that enforcers aren't ones to report concussions to their teams, because doing so would mean losing one's spot in the lineup for a few games and opening the door for another hungry fourth-liner to take their place.

So they stay silent on brain injuries...until we hear them well after their playing days, talking about memory loss and joining concussion lawsuits.

But according to this study: the long-term effects of fighting on a player's brain are frightening, but more concussions are caused by high-velocity hits during play than in a fight.

But other times, the fighters themselves mutually decide to stop the fight. Sometimes this is due to injury, but mostly this is due to exhaustion.

"A lot of time you're looking at him. If you fight at the end of a shift, you can tell you're tired, and you just kind of know that the fight's done," said Bissonnette.

THE END OF THE FIGHTING

Fighting in the NHL declined every year from 2009 through 2014. While there have been rules put in place to curb it—the instigator rule in 1992, for example, which assessed an additional penalty to the player who started the fisticuffs—the most significant legislation to lessen fighting were the rules changes after the 2005 lockout that made the game faster and more offensive.

Suddenly, the five-minute-a-night goon on the fourth line who was great with his fists but lousy with his skates was a relic. Many were cut from teams and drifted into NHL history.

But even without rules changes, fighting is also leaving the game organically. It's actually a bit of a "trickle up" effect: as more lower tiers of hockey pass anti-fighting rules, more players come up the ranks not having fights as a regular occurrence. The Ontario Hockey League, for example, has restrictions on the number of times a player can fight during a season before facing supplemental discipline.

So while fighting is still very much a part of the culture, its regularity is not part of the culture of future generations of NHLers.

Will the NHL ever ban it?

Morbid as this sounds, it would probably take a fighting-related death.

Even with the CTE crisis and concussion drama surrounding the game, the NHL doesn't view fighting in the same way it does in-game shots to the head. The league still sees fighting as some level of deterrence for that other violence.

That's something many enforcers cite, too: What rises up if fighting is gone? What takes its place as a form of revenge or intimidation? Stick work? Elbows to the head?

"Intimidation is part of hockey life and fighting has a place in our sport. It keeps the game in check with fewer stick incidents and runs at guys, and it's a great release valve in a pressure-filled contest," wrote Severyn. "The dirtiest, nastiest, most dangerous hockey I've played was in leagues that didn't have fighting."

But there's also the elephant landing body blows in the corner of the room: the NHL keeps fighting around because the majority of its die-hard customers want it in the game, and that's the reason the league continues to promote something that is, by definition, against the rules.

"People forget…fans, the energy in the building, creates a lot of that," said Bissonnette. "Look at how the networks promote the game. They'll call it rivalry night, show a goal, show a fight, show a big save, and show 18 other fights."

HOW NOT TO HIT

The NHL's Department of Player Safety exists not only to punish those players who step over the line of legality, but to attempt to change behavior among the game's physical players.

Its genesis was three incidents that impacted the league. There was Mike Richards' targeted hit to the head of David Booth that put the then-Panthers forward on a stretcher. There was Matt Cooke's hit to the head of Marc Savard, ending the Bruins star's career with a concussion. And there were the hits by Dave Steckel and Victor Hedman on Sidney

Crosby, which put the Penguins star out of action for months and sparked a wide-ranging debate about how to protect the league's best players.

So the process began to re-educate players on how to hit each other. Which might sound nonsensical within the context of a contact sport, but was essential given the direction both the NHL and society were headed.

The first and most obvious move: banning hits in which the principal point of contact was the head. Rule 48 was passed in 2011, banning "lateral, blindside, or east-west hits." The rule was tweaked over the next two seasons, including the NHL taking the word "targeting" out of the language and going for a more general and sweeping "a hit resulting in contact with an opponent's head where the head was the main point of contact and such contact to the head was avoidable."

So when is contact avoidable? Good question. The NHL applies a test to determine whether contact with the head is actually an illegal check to the head.

First, was it just a matter of poor timing, of an unfortunate series of events that led to a player's eggs getting scrambled? To that end, did the player getting hit put himself in a vulnerable spot that turned a full-body check into one that made contact with the head?

Second, for the player delivering the hit: did he materially change the angle of his body or his approach on the hit in a way that significantly contributed to contact being made with the head?

The onus is almost always going to be on the hitter. The basic mantra from the NHL is to not deliver a hit that doesn't need to be delivered.

Take charging for example. NHL rules stipulate that "a minor or major penalty shall be imposed on a player who skates or jumps into or charges an opponent in any manner."

"Jumps into" is pretty straightforward: some dummy decides to go Air Jordan to inflict damage on an opponent by "launching" up and into a player's head. But the nuance of the rule is this: just because a player "launches" doesn't mean that it's a penalty or a suspendable offense. A player can launch into an opponent, but not up and into his head. That could be a clean hit.

The "skates" part is always the trickier one, and that goes for charging or boarding, a penalty given to a player "who checks or pushes a defenseless opponent in such a manner that causes the opponent to hit or impact the boards violently or dangerously. The severity of the penalty, based upon the impact with the boards, shall be at the discretion of the Referee."

The severity of a hit is determined by the damage it causes to an opponent, and the violent nature of the check. The distances traveled for a hit are always the first harbinger of illegality: if a hitter has taken several strides from the other end of the ice before delivering the hit, it's going to be regarded as illegal. Similarly, if there is a violent impact against the boards on the hit, it's going to result in a boarding major.

Hitting has changed dramatically in the last 20 years, as the days of Scott Stevens trying to (legally, at the time) decapitate foes are long gone.

But much the way cockroaches will still be scurrying around after the sun explodes, pests and rats will still populate the National Hockey League, just like they always have.

» HOCKEY'S MOST HEINOUS ON-ICE CRIMES

The NHL's Department of Player Safety was founded in 2011 as a way for the NHL to better assign supplemental discipline to injurious players and to educate those players on what not to do on the ice to injure their fellow man.

Did it work? Well, it added uniformity to the league's suspension policies and decreased the number of call-out-the-stretcher hits we've seen in the league. But hockey remains an inherently violent sport played by some inherently violent men. Player safety can be paramount, but there will always be risks to that safety.

Here are some of the most dastardly acts seen on the ice.

Blindside Hits
Any hit that arrives outside of a player's sightlines, usually targeting the head.

Rule 48 in the NHL rulebook greatly lessened the amount of blindside hits we see in the league, but they still happen. And when they do, it remains one of the most deplorable plays a player can make.

"I've been in that situation where I could lay a guy out, and I just kind of bend down instead and let my ass hit them," said enforcer Paul Bissonnette. "I want to do it. But I know it's not honest to do it. And plus, I don't want to lose money."

Slew Foot
A player uses his leg to kick his opponent's feet out from underneath him while pulling the opponent's upper body back toward the ice.

This is just a deplorable play, and frequently accompanied by something along the lines of "the kind of thing we don't want in our game." Just the rattiest of rat-like behavior.

The Spear
As Justin Bourne once called it: "The drive-by shooting of hate hockey."

The spear is a gutless move, which is ironic considering the stick's target is usually right in his opponent's gut. It's an act of cowardice, using one's stick rather than engaging physically with the other player. And it's an act of irresponsibility, as hockey players are entrusted *not* to weaponize the weapons they legally carry. Yet there's Mr. Bravery, wielding a harpoon years after the Whalers relocated.

The Spear in the Junk
Like a spear, except providing legal grounds for being stuffed in a small rocket and shot into the sun for one's lack of human decency.

The Butt-End
The nasty cousin to the spear, the butt-end of the stick to an opponent's face usually occurs off a face-off or in the corner, as one player attempts to ward off the other with a handle to the face, and then acts like it's an unfortunate mistake. Hey, no hard feelings...now, where's that tooth?

Boarding in the Numbers
In youth hockey, they put a giant STOP patch on the backs of jerseys to make sure no one is hit squarely in the numbers while facing the boards. That could work in the NHL, as long as the sign lights up and shoots sparks or something, because these guys shamelessly hit each other in the digits along the boards all the time. Because, hey, it's the other guy's spine that might snap, so why should they care?

One caveat: players will sometimes turn their backs to hits in order to draw a penalty, which is all the proof you need that fame is a hell of a drug.

THE RATS

My favorite player growing up had 379 career goals, 786 career points, four Stanley Cup rings, a Conn Smythe Trophy, and, at one point in his career, was considered the single worst human being on the face of the earth.

Claude Lemieux's name adorned the back of my jersey, which in some parts of North America was grounds for being institutionalized. He was a cheap-shot artist who turtled when asked to answer for his sins with his fists. He once sparked a blood feud between Colorado and Detroit after hitting the Red Wings' Kris Draper from behind into the boards and shattering his face. He was called a cancer in the locker room.

And yet I understood what he was: the uber-rat, a player who could annoy the hell of you with his mouth, fists, stick, and elbows all game, and then crush your spirit by scoring the game-winning goal.

To me, that's why not all rats are created equal. Many teams employ marginal talents whose job entails hounding players exponentially more accomplished than they are. They skate their eight minutes a night, pick up their penalty minutes, and run their mouths like they're at an open mic at the Comedy Cellar.

But guys like Claude Lemieux, Esa Tikkanen, Chris Pronger, and Brad Marchand were a better class of criminal. Rats, for sure, but ones who would add that extra layer of frustration because they were darn good hockey players. OK, in Pronger's case, potentially a sociopath, but a sociopath with a Calder, a Norris, and nearly two Conn Smythes in losing efforts!

The lament from old-school hockey guys like Brian Burke is that the rats are running the ship without fighters around to drive them into the sea.

"I don't see accountability or respect in the game right now, and that troubles me," he said in 2012. "There are some middleweights who fight and they're not the rats and they back up their teammates. Would those guys do those things if there was retribution or accountability in the game? I'm not so sure."

Here's the thing: hockey will always have its nasty bits. Guys like Burke know that rodent-like behavior has existed for decades, as has the alleged "enforcement" that allegedly keeps it at bay, allegedly. It's a constant balance between honor and dishonor, respect and disrespect. It may dissipate because of shifting norms, player safety concerns, and changes to the rules. It may transform, as it did when the new rules made the Neaderthalic pugilist extinct.

But fighting, gouging, slashing, poking, prodding, yapping…it's always going to be the underbelly of the game. And outwardly or secretly, we'll love it.

CHAPTER 9

A DAY IN THE LIFE OF A PLAYER

(National Hockey League defenseman Karl Alzner is one of the most interesting and introspective players I've ever interviewed. I spoke with him during the 2014–15 Washington Capitals season to get a glimpse of what life is like for a player away from the rink.

"My life became different with a newborn, so 8:00 AM is sleeping in a bit after a home game the night before. First, I punish a half a pot of coffee. I'll flick on the news, see what's going on there, and then I have a few apps on my phone that I hit. Trivia Crack. I play a lot of the guys on my team.

"After that, it's straight to the rink. And I don't have to bring anything, because it's all there. Including more coffee. You can just roll out of bed and head to the rink if that's the kind of guy you are. The single guys. Or the guys who really need their sleep.

"Morning skate, on a game day, is 10:15 AM. On an off-day, between 10:30 to 11:00. You have to be there an hour before practice, but typically guys get there up to two hours before. I get there, have breakfast, and sit in the trainers' room, getting any injury rehab if I need it.

"We'll have a meeting at about 9:30 AM in a theater at our practice facility. We also have computers set up where you can watch all your shifts from the night before, if we had a game. Then you get a workout in until about half an hour before practice. All the guys are different, but I stay away from any extra cardio exercises during the season. Light weights or mobility; I'm a guy who likes to work on his core, work on balance.

"This is usually around the time where guys get ping-pong games in, or right after the skate. But it's weird…once November hits, we don't play any ping-pong until it gets sunny out again. We just talked about it the other day. It's so weird. I do not get it.

"You tape your stick, get on your gear, and hit the ice. We do a lot of the same drills, and it can drag on at times. Mostly working on regrouping, playing in the neutral zone, and odd-man rushes. For the defensemen, it's our coverage and our work in the corners. But they're good for keeping you sharp. We'll throw in ones that might be specific to a team we're playing that night—like if they have good defensive-zone coverage, we'll work on our forecheck. If we're practicing it, there's probably a reason we're practicing it.

"The intensity depends on how the games are going. If the coaches aren't happy, you go a little harder. In some drills, you have to battle. So some guys get hit in the head with an elbow or a guy gets tripped or slashed. You get frustrated. But there haven't been any fights in our practices. We have seen two guys slash the heck out of each other. You just sorta laugh, because you can see it coming.

"We'll skate for 30 to 45 minutes, and then you just horse around for 15 or so. Working on your shot. Playing keep-away with someone.

"No one cares who the last player on the ice is. Players take care of their bodies in different ways, and that sometimes means getting off the ice as fast as possible. It's usually the young guys who are on the ice the longest. Because they have to pick up pucks.

"After practice, you don't have any more team commitments for a while. Some guys get a cold bath or stretch. Some guys play more ping-pong. On a game day, we'll do more video work, including extra work for the penalty kill. This year, we're doing a bit more: 25 minutes to a half hour, when in the past it was about 10 minutes.

"At 11:15, on a game day, we'll have our pregame meal. And that'll be the only meal we have until after the game, typically. If you're hungry, there's some bagels and stuff at the arena, and little snacks, like oatmeal. Then, after the game, we'll have steak and fries. Because we're meat-and-potatoes kind of people. We've occasionally had lamb, and the guys are really big fans of that. But you just want to get something into your body. You don't care what it is.

"On a game day, most guys will take a nap in between the skate and the game. I've been trying to phase mine out, so I have a few hours to take care of some things or be with family. Some guys take two-hour naps. Other guys take 30 minutes. I'm more of the 30-minute type when I need it. But some days, there's nothing you can do to fall asleep.

"I get to the arena for a home game at 4:15 PM. Hop in a car with the guys at about 3:50. The carpool is determined by which of our wives isn't coming that night to the game; that guy is the driver.

"It's so weird when we carpool. It's me, [defensemen] John Carlson, Brooks Orpik, and Matt Niskanen, and [forwards] Troy Brouwer and Nicklas Backstrom. We all live really close to each other. But when we have to take a longer road trip, or drive to the airport, it's just me and the defensemen. The forwards drive themselves.

"When we get to the arena, every guy has his own routine from about 4:30 until 6:00. I hot tub, and then I get my sticks ready. Cut 'em down, tape 'em. That usually takes me 15 minutes. I stretch, do a snatch in the gym and some balance work, and then chat with the guys while the power play [unit] has its meeting.

"We do our team meeting, which is our coach coming in and reminding us about what we need to focus on and what the opponent's going to try to do. After that, some guys go to the gym and guys like me go play soccer for about 20 minutes in the hallway. I head back to the room, hit the trainer again, gear up 15 minutes before warmup, and then we get going.

"I should say that everyone has their own intense pregame rituals. Matt Hendricks was the most intense I'd ever seen. He would go around the room, go up to each player, and say the same thing to everyone before every game. He had a few one-liners he'd hit certain guys with, just to make everyone laugh and bring some noise in the room. I didn't have one. He'd just tap me on my pads. But I didn't feel left out.

"After the game, we come off the ice and have a quick pow-wow in the dressing room with the coaches. If we've won, there's a lot of music. It's a lot more fun to win. Then we do our media obligations, hit the gym again for a workout—it's never mandatory, but encouraged. You head to the trainer if you need to, but now you're on your own time. So I try to hit the cold tub one more time, shower, and then head home.

"I usually get home around an hour after the game. Then I grab a Coors Light, sit in front of the TV, and talk to my wife. I usually won't get to bed until around 1:00 AM on a game night.

"For a road trip…it's actually really great when we don't have to practice in the morning, and we can drive right to the airport. That way when we get back in the middle of the night, we can drive home. But to get to the plane, we have to drive out to Dulles Airport [in Virginia] because Reagan National has a curfew. So a lot of guys end up living out near Dulles.

"The timing of things is similar. The morning skate gets pushed back an hour on the road. You come in so late that it messes up your sleep. You can sleep on the plane, but you don't want to sleep on the plane, you know? You want to get some binge-watching in. Or play cards. I'm a TV guy, but when I do play cards, I play crib. But there are only about six guys who play cards on the plane now, and when they do, they play Snarples. It's a card game you'll find on every team. There's actually an app for it, and the icon is an image of a hockey player.

"Hotel life might sound nice to some people, but you get sick of it about halfway through the season. It's not fun to live out of a suitcase. You get in, kill an hour and a half playing on the computer or watching TV, and then meet in the lobby around 6:00 PM for a team meal. Some guys like certain things—fish, steaks—and we go out in groups based on that. It's funny, we come off the road and the only thing we want is home cooking, and the only thing our wives and girlfriends want is to get out of the house and grab something to eat.

"It used to be that you had to room with someone on the road, and it was usually someone who had the same schedule as you do. But now we room alone. You have 30-year-old guys with families who want to FaceTime for an hour, and you don't want to do that with a roommate. The only guys who have roommates are guys on entry-level contracts, not us veterans, which is great. I like to fall asleep with the TV on. If someone doesn't like that, it's not going to be good.

"It's not easy to play road games. You get out of your routine. But what really sucks is being alone, being away from family. You get a little time for sightseeing and things on the road, but you don't really do much unless family is in town.

"If you're going to a town where you have family…well, you have to be ready to buy a whole lotta tickets. The last two years, we did suites in Vancouver and Calgary. That's 40-something tickets, in two of the most expensive NHL cities. So as we like to say, you're playing for free that night.

"You call into [the opponent's] ticket office and see what they have. My parents or my in-laws will usually call. I guess one of the things about road life that people don't understand is that when people ask, 'Hey, can you hook me up with four tickets in Toronto?' and we're like…'Uh, those tickets are $300 a pop. I'm not sure,' we're not trying to be [jerks]. It's not like we can just go to the arena and reach into a pile of tickets for the night. It adds up pretty quick.

NHL REGULAR-SEASON TRAVEL MILEAGE, BY TEAM

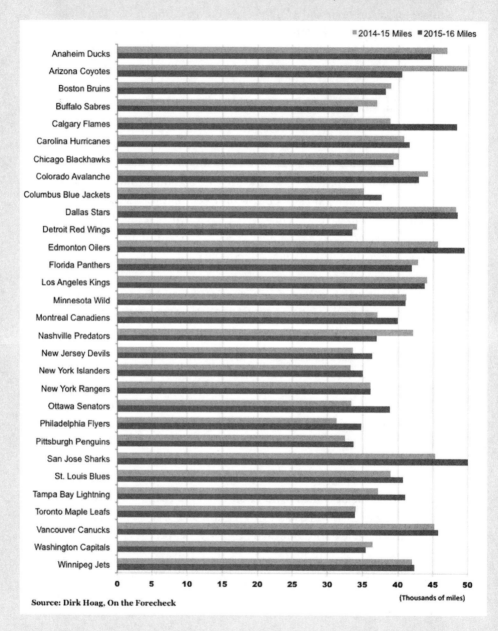

Source: Dirk Hoag, On the Forecheck

"Life as a player isn't too far off from what I imagined it would be. The one big misconception about it is that when you make the NHL, it's all happiness. Everything's easy. But the pressure is so much more. The expectations are so much more. There's so much more expected from you. And you think about it all the time. And you hear about it all the time, from media outlets and social media. It's a 24/7 type of thing.

"And it's almost a 12-month-a-year job. After the season, you meet with coaches and management. They tell you what they liked, and they tell you what you need to work on. Those fun things—what you need to get better at in the summer. The trainers do the same thing.

"As you're meeting with the media for the last time that season, you're saying good-bye to teammates. And so the mood is never that great. You're trying not to be a big downer about it if you didn't win the playoffs, but you can't help it. Some guys leave town quickly. Other guys stick around and try to do stuff with other teammates before everyone else leaves.

"As a player, you know you're never bringing the exact same team back. It's a tough time of year. You're upset because you didn't win, but at the same time you want to enjoy the last days you have with your teammates. You almost feel guilty when you're at a baseball game with them or playing golf, because you don't feel like you should be having fun. At the same time, you have to enjoy your time with your friends, and then your family in the summer, as you try to come back next fall with a clean slate mentally."

CHAPTER 10

THE MANAGEMENT

Secret deals! Dramatic decisions! Dictating the very future of a given franchise! Building Rome in a day, or more likely utilizing a job-securing five-year plan!

Ah yes, the thrill-a-minute life of an NHL general manger.

"Actually, it's boring as hell."

That's Brad Treliving. He's the general manager of the Calgary Flames, after having served as the assistant GM under Don Maloney with the Arizona Coyotes for 11 years. There are two types of general managers in the league: those who cut their teeth as NHL players, and guys like Treliving, whose highest level of pro hockey in a nine-year career as a defenseman was 15 games in the American Hockey League.

(He's perhaps most famous for being the son of Canadian millionaire Jim Treliving, who founded Boston Pizza and starred on *Dragon's Den*, better known as *Shark Tank* in the U.S. because, by and large, Americans are more afraid of shark attacks than dragon attacks, despite what we have seen from Drogan, Viserion, and Rhaegal on HBO's *Game of Thrones*.)

Sensing he wasn't destined to become Bobby Orr in his later years, Treliving co-founded the Western Professional Hockey League in 1996 and orchestrated its merger with the Central Hockey League in 2001, before joining the Coyotes to be Maloney's right-hand man in player personnel and to run the AHL San Antonio Rampage.

"You guys are going to be like, 'I don't want to live this guy's life.' It's somewhere in between misery and boredom," he said.

While it's not exactly *that* dire, he's not exactly that far off either. NHL general managers have to be masters of several domains. Their days are spent communicating with staff, coaches, and their peers. Their jobs are as much about the day-to-day operations of a multi-million-dollar business as they are acting as an amateur fortune teller.

"The biggest challenge is to stay ahead of what's happening rather than react to it," said Treliving.

So what do these rumple-suited men with the corner offices do to run their teams?

A DAY IN THE LIFE

It's rare that general managers start their day with something monumental, although then-Capitals GM George McPhee did fire coach Bruce Boudreau at around 6:15 AM back in 2011. Which stinks, given Bruce's affinity for breakfast, our most important meal of the day.

Rather, general managers usually arrive at a team's practice facility before the players do in order to get a status report on the roster.

Let's take an injured player, for example. The front office staff consults the medical staff about the player's status, and the likelihood he'll play that night depending on how he looks in practice. Then they'll develop a backup plan: how that player will be replaced in the lineup if he can't go, and whether that absence would necessitate a call-up from the American Hockey League.

The AHL is a pro league, and it sometimes gets overlooked as a developmental league. There's actually a rule in place that 13 skaters in every AHL game have to be "developmental talent," meaning that 12 must have played in 260 or fewer professional games (in any league) and one must have played in 320 or fewer games. Those eligibility numbers are tabulated at the start of each season.

Players in the NHL are on either two-way or one-way contracts. The former gives a player a different wage if he's in the NHL or the minor leagues, significantly more when he's with the big club; the latter means he gets paid his NHL salary no matter where he's playing, but he must clear waivers before he can play in the AHL.

Let's say that player is deemed too injured to play. The first move is to place him on injured reserve, which mandates that the player stay out of the lineup for at least a week. That designation opens up a roster spot for another player to be added, so the GM calls up a player from the AHL. That can begin a chain reaction, as the AHL team then calls up a player from the ECHL as a replacement, and the ECHL may seek to bring in another player to supplant that one.

That business handled, it's then time to watch practice while huddling with the rest of the front office. After that's done, it's time for some powwows with the coaching staff. The amount of advice given here depends on what kind of working relationship the GM and coach have. Most consult on lineups, sharing what they witnessed in practice and what the upcoming opponent will attempt to throw at them. Others will engage in full-on debates about game-planning for the night's contest.

You'll notice we haven't described a lot of interaction with players, and that's because there isn't. The general manager will typically have two or three leaders in the locker room—some might say snitches—that he can rely on to measure the pulse of the team. But a player going to the general manager for a hockey-related matter is a bit like complaining to the CEO of the burger chain about the taste of your fries: there are several layers of leadership that a player can opt to communicate with and through before getting to the GM.

One of those layers? Player agents. General managers speak with agents every day. Sometimes it's for contract matters, but most of the time it's to provide updates or clarifications on their clients' playing time or role on the team—especially if there's been a demotion for that player.

"A lot of times I'll give the agent a heads-up if a player is demoted. A lot of it has less to do with the agent and more about how much maintenance the agent has to do with the player," said Kyle Dubas, assistant general manager of the Toronto Maple Leafs. "A lot of people will say an agent is a pain in the ass, but I don't think it's true. An agent meets the client's demands. If he's high-maintenance and whiny, you'll hear from the agent."

The general managers are also in constant contact with other GMs, looking to address a team need or see what another team might need in the future.

A general manager's day is a constant state of player evaluation. Along with agents and other GMs, he'll speak to his own departments to learn more about the players on the roster and in the system.

THE STAFF CONSTRUCTION

The leader of the player personnel staff is the team president, for all intents and purposes the proxy for ownership who oversees the entire operation.

It's a job with sweeping scope and powers, literally touching on every aspect of the team operations on and off the ice.

Take someone like Ted Black of the Buffalo Sabres. Formerly the senior vice president and general manager of a regional sports network in Pittsburgh, he was brought on by owner Terry Pegula in 2010 to oversee…well, everything the Sabres do.

He was charged with hiring the leadership group for the team's various departments. He's the point man for corporate partnerships, team advertising, negotiations with the National Hockey League, working with the Sabres' rights-holders on television and the radio, fan relations, and ticket sales.

Black, who was replaced as team president in 2015, frequently played an uncomfortable role for the Sabres. For example, in 2013, Black was grilled by reporters who questioned where his boss was as the Sabres ended a disastrous season.

"Terry hired me to run the business and speak for the business," Black said. "He hired Darcy [Regier] to run the hockey operation and speak for the hockey operations. He has a high level of trust…and he has empowered us to do that. So that's our role. Terry's role is more of being a typical owner."

The team president might also be the general manager, but typically the GM is the next link in the chain of command.

I've always been fascinated with general managers, and not just because I was the kid who enjoyed making trades on video games as much as scoring the game-winning goal. The managerial approach of the GM sets the tone for the entire organization.

Lou Lamoriello was, perhaps, the most myopic and mettlesome executive I've ever covered in sports. For years he was the New Jersey Devils' general manager as well as its team president, so there wasn't an aspect of the franchise he didn't have his hands on, for better or for worse.

For better: his bold decisions to form the core of that championship team. Asking an arbitrator for Scott Stevens after the Blues signed away Brendan Shanahan. Hiring Jacques Lemaire and Larry Robinson from

One of my favorite aspects of the old-school EA Sports hockey games was the ability to be the general manager. And by that I mean do the things that general managers do, which is to crush the lives of grown men by trading them away from their loved ones in an effort to win a big silver doorstop in June.

Those video games offered me the chance to make a blockbuster deal to improve my team, but with one caveat: if the computer AI felt that the abilities of the players made for a realistic trade, a voice trumpeted "TRADE ACCEPTED"; but if you were trying to game the system with an unfair trade—Mario Lemieux for a shoebox of expired Burger King coupons, for example—the voice would disapprovingly lament "TRADE DENIED."

This is what I always figured Dan Ages, associate counsel for the NHL, did on a daily basis, up until the trade deadline. His department facilitates trade calls between teams, and acts as the auditor to make sure every detail is covered and every restriction is adhered to.

A trade call is usually initiated by one team, either through a call or a fax (yes, a fax) to the league offices in Toronto. Ages' team gathers all the necessary documentation, including the player contracts, and fills in the blanks on a "trade call form" from Central Registry that resembles something you might find in a doctor's waiting room.

Next, the two teams are conference-called in with the NHL. One team announces the trade, and the audit process begins. Ages or his team will ask about:

The 50 Man Reserve List: Teams have a 50-contract maximum for players signed to NHL deals, including those on injured reserve. A trade can only be completed if both sides have room under the maximum. Another wrinkle: teams have to have two goalies on their NHL roster at all times. If you trade one, you need to tell the league where another one's coming from (i.e., the minors).

The 50-contract limit doesn't apply in the summer, which is why some deals wait until the draft to be completed. (Ages and his team are on-site to approve trades made on the draft floor.) Teams can also go over the salary cap in the summer, which brings us to...

Salary Cap Compliance: Ages said that teams don't make the trade call if they don't already have the cap numbers worked out, whether it's how much room each team has to take on contracts or how much cap space one team seeks to retain in a trade to make it fit under the cap.

(Teams can't absorb more than 50 percent of the player's annual salary, and can only retain salary on up to three contracts they traded away. They also can only have 15 percent of their cap space used up by that retained salary, aka dead space.)

The salary issues in trades have cleared up through the NHL's many work stoppages. In the 2012 lockout, for example, the league ruled that a team trading for a player assumes all of his bonus clauses, even if he scores 49 points with one team and one point with another to trigger a 50-point salary bonus.

Working within the cap gets easier as the season goes on, as salaries for traded players are prorated to the end of the season.

Draft Picks: The NHL has a large database of the draft picks for the next several seasons and which teams own them. So, if a pick is moved, there's a way to cross-reference that the team actually owns that pick and that there aren't any restrictions on it. This is also where conditions are placed on draft picks, i.e., how a third-round pick can become a second-round pick if a team wins a conference title. Glad someone is keeping track of these things; I always just assumed they used Wikipedia like we did.

No-Move Clauses: If a player has a full no-movement clause, the team has to get him to sign a waiver to release it from that contractual obligation. If the player has a limited no-move clause—listing several teams he can't be traded to, for example—then the team just has to follow those guidelines laid out in their contract.

Fun fact: some players have no-trade clauses in which they submit lists to their teams each season, and some players have contracts that detail the teams they don't want to be traded to, from the time they sign the contract. Which is silly, considering how many worst-to-firsts we see in the NHL.

Physicals: Not every trade requires a physical, but many of them do. They're conducted as soon as a player is on-site for a team, and a player may not take part in any activities with the team until he passes that physical. If he fails it...well, "TRADE DENIED."

Most trade calls take around 15 minutes. Trades made before 5:00 PM ET have teams assuming contracts that day; anything later, and it's the following day.

Ages said the NHL trade deadline is a different animal. He enlists extra help from NHL Central Registry to man the phones, due to the sheer volume of trades. The majority of them are completed by 1:30 PM ET, but some teams have filed trades at 2:59 PM ET, one minute before the deadline.

Ages and his crew also work NHL free agency, approving the contracts of players who sign in the summer. Again, the CBA's restrictions on contracts have made life easier for them, as there are no longer any 17-year deals with dramatically fluctuating annual salary numbers to suss out.

"The biggest challenge in free agency," Ages said, "is that some guys don't have fax machines in their cottages."

the Montreal Canadiens to graft that franchise's identity onto one that Wayne Gretzky once referred to as "Mickey Mouse." Embracing their defense-first philosophy that came to represent roughly two decades of Devils hockey.

For worse: as both the head of hockey operations and the team's off-ice initiatives, Lamoriello infamously was reluctant to market his players and his team during its three-Stanley-Cup-win era. The thought was that it would be for the betterment of the team's on-ice focus to have their profiles low; yet those low profiles, combined with the team's nap-inducing defensive style, failed to capitalize on the momentum of their championship wins. Empty seats were found at the majority of Devils home games, even after the team relocated to Newark.

Oh, it didn't stop there with the micro-management. Lamoriello would change the colors of the team's jerseys, but not the logo itself. (He would also steadfastly refuse to create a third jersey for the team; can you imagine how much money the Devils left on the table by foregoing an all-black jersey with a heavy metal Satan head on the front?) He influenced game-night operations, including musical choices that provoked fans to create vulgar chants. He would offer strict policies on social media.

His most infamous obsession? Hair.

Even back when he was the head coach at Providence College in the 1970s, Lamoriello demanded that his players not have a single strand of hair touching one's ear. Which led to a bit of hilarity when Providence played the cadets of West Point, who told then-Friars player Brian Burke, "Hey, man, what's with the hair? We have to do this. What's with you guys?'"

To his final days as GM of the Devils, Lamoriello didn't allow facial hair on his players and coaches. "The word is called *tradition*. That's the identity of the Devils organization," he said in 2015. "Those are part of the systemic points that have given us our identity, like our home and away jerseys. Whether you look at the Yankees or the old Montreal

Canadiens and their identity, this is the identity of the Devils. I look at it as something the players, and hopefully the fans, take pride in."

Like we said, the general manager sets the tone. Whether it's what style the organization decides to play, or what style the organization decides for their players' follicles.

The next link in the chain is the assistant general manager, and that role varies for every team, as do their numbers.

One assistant general manager will be tasked with directly assisting the general manager on all matters pertaining to the NHL team, from player signings to trades.

Another assistant general manager will be charged with the development of team prospects in the minor leagues and in junior hockey, checking on their development and constantly evaluating their progress. This role can also fall to a director of player development and/or a director of minor league operations.

Another option, one employed by teams such as the Tampa Bay Lightning and Toronto Maple Leafs, is to have an assistant general manager serve as the general manager of the team's American Hockey League affiliate, bringing together the two organizations in a synergistic way (and greasing the tracks for players to flow back and forth from the organizations more easily). Other teams, including the St. Louis Blues, choose to keep the two roles separate.

There's usually a developmental staff that looks at ways to optimize player development throughout the franchise's system, attempting to improve the tools at every level to help them excel. This includes new coaching techniques, equipment, and fitness requirements.

A team's scouting department has several tasks at hand. Scouts are called on to look at teams who come through their cities so coaches have a scouting report on those foes. At the same time, they're keeping an eye on trade targets.

The director of professional scouting sits at the top of the food chain. He's responsible for organizing the scouting staff and keeping everyone on the same page in terms of the attributes the organization wants in its players. He reports to the director of player personnel.

The European head scout manages scouting reports from Euro-based scouts and coordinates their activities. Below him are regional scouts who follow NHL and AHL teams, and the Euro pro leagues.

The amateur scouting apparatus mirrors this setup. The differences between amateur and pro scouts are obvious—one is looking for prospects to sign or draft and develop, the other is looking to add established players to the current roster. But the essential variance between the two is that one deals in potential and one deals in the actual.

An amateur scout is evaluating the skill sets of the players, their possibility for growth, and how they project once they're added to the lineup. The pro scout understands what the player is; the task is seeing how his skills fit with the roster and the talent on the team. That includes evaluating their current situation with a team and why he might be available—is it a problem with chemistry? With ice time and usage?

Scouts are constantly looking at and re-evaluating potential draft picks around North America. They're given a list of organizational needs and then sent out to locate players who can fill those needs via the draft. They watch the young players, and then interview people around those players, such as coaches and trainers.

Scouting is a thorough process. Teams employ something called "cross checking" (because it's hockey, I guess) in which one scout will confirm another scout's work by laying eyes on the players they're scouting. Teams like the Maple Leafs only have four full-time scouts in Europe, and they will frequently check each other's reports in person.

"There's so much we can do at the NHL level with video and analysis, but it's important for scouts to still go to games and look at things the team is really trying to vet about players," said Dubas.

Of course, once you find players, you have to sign players, and that's when the salary cap comes into play.

A team's "capologist" will likely be an assistant to the general manager, in charge of following the day-to-day cap number for his team and for those around the NHL, attempting to identify which teams could be in trouble and hence might need to dump players.

Remember: the salary cap is still a fairly recent thing, in NHL terms, having been born out of the 2005 NHL lockout. (The one that cost us a season, just so we could then lose half a season roughly eight years later.) Teams had to create new positions within their management team in order to have someone monitoring the cap space; or, in the case of Frank Provenzano, they had to add another job to someone's plate.

Provenzano was an assistant general manager with the Dallas Stars, and was their "capologist." Except please never refer to him as a capologist, because he believes it makes him sound like a mushroom farmer.

Provenzano succinctly explained the role to *The Globe & Mail* while working for the Stars: "In hockey, if you only base your analysis on goals, you're going to miss 98 percent of the other things that are happening that have value. So what are those things, and what value do they have, and then how do you translate that value into your decision making—into dollars. That is the stuff people like myself do. It's not contract law. It's that."

If that sounds a little "moneypuck," that's because there's plenty of crossover between the world of hockey analytics and economics. The driving force behind the embracing of "fancy stats" has always been a way to evaluate the true value of players, and in some cases find cheaper, more effective versions of higher-priced players.

Increasingly, the last part of a team's front office is an analytic group or individual. Most teams now have someone who watches out for advanced stat trends among players and within the team.

In some cases, the analytics are more completely embraced. Some teams track them in real time during games, and then make that information available to coaches via any mobile device.

But overall, the analytics are usually collected and presented to team executives during the season and especially in the off-season, when possession stats and other metrics are used to determine which players are worth throwing money at.

It's not uniform just yet—some teams ignore them, others give them lip service to look like they're with the cool kids.

You can usually tell which team is which after someone makes a god-awful trade.

THE PLAYER PERSONNEL

A general manager's primary function is determining who is, or who is not, on the team.

It's a constant state of evaluation. Players whose contracts are up at the end of the season may choose to negotiate in-season or not, but their performance is being evaluated every game, and the performances of comparable teammates and opponents are being evaluated as well.

Even if they can read the writing on the wall, most free-agent players aren't sure of their fates with the club until postseason meetings with coaches and management. The situation changes for every general manager. Some will allow players to test the market in the hopes they'll re-sign for a hometown discount; others will see their free agents bolt come July.

Free agency is a bit of a "changing on the fly" situation. It's earned the nickname "Frenzy" considering how many signings happen, and how much teams have to change plans in an instant when they do.

The trade market is, despite what we see on Deadline Day, more of a long game.

The groundwork for most trades is laid early in the season, the back burner filled with possibilities depending on how the season goes. One NHL front office man told me that for every one trade that goes down, there are three that imploded.

It's become increasingly harder to make a move in the NHL. The salary cap necessitates creativity in making the money work, but sometimes it just can't. Season-reshaping injuries come out of nowhere. Some teams have money issues. Some teams are much more willing to deal when they're losing, and then completely snub their potential trade partners when they're winning.

If there's paralysis in the trade market, it can come from sheer over-cautiousness. No one wants to get burned in a trade. No one wants to be made to look the fool while the other guy hoists the Cup.

This is partially because general managers know they're essentially like film directors: no matter how many blockbusters you've made, no matter how many theaters you've filled, one smoldering bomb could define your career. George McPhee, for example, helped build a consistent contender with the Washington Capitals that won several division titles. But he'll also always be the guy who traded a can't-miss blue-chipper named Filip Forsberg for veteran winger Martin Erat, who had demanded a trade from Nashville.

A few months later Erat demanded a trade from the Capitals, too.

It was only the second major trade between McPhee and Nashville GM David Poile, the man he replaced at the top of the Capitals. And he got burned.

That's why you frequently see trades that involve two teams that are "trading partners," i.e., the general managers know, like, and trust each other.

Whether it's trades or cuts or signings, the words of Brad Treliving linger: "The biggest challenge is to stay ahead of what's happening rather than react to it."

There are two types of general managers: the reactive ones, who try to harness the lightning-in-a-bottle of a contender and then try to climb out of the cap mess they've made for themselves; and the proactive ones, who make tough decisions on veteran players with bloated salaries; who make bold moves to improve the team, but only when it's ready to contend; and who do all this without handing over picks and prospects that undermine the future.

The former might hoist the Cup if the planets align; the latter wants to challenge for the Cup on an annual basis in perpetuity.

"Getting good is hard," said Treliving. "It's a process. You have to build a strong base first."

THE DREAM TEAM

So, what are the keys to a successful roster?

Drafting
Dear lord, drafting. Not every team gets the lottery balls bouncing its way. And not every GM has the luxury of even being in the lottery each year. So the key becomes drafting well, especially outside of the first round; and the key becomes finding players outside the draft, either from Europe or toiling in someone else's minor league system.

But also…

That Delicate Balance Between Patience and Blind Loyalty

When teams give up on good young players, trading them out of frustration or for trading's sake, that's an express train to regret. Building a core, keeping that core together, and having the patience to allow for growing pains is a slow ride to success.

But there will come times when cutting bait makes sense. Dean Lombardi of the Los Angeles Kings had to make that call. He traded defenseman Jack Johnson, 25 and playing well over 23 minutes a game, to Columbus for Jeff Carter. He traded Wayne Simmonds, a 23-year-old power forward, and Brayden Schenn, arguably the best prospect in the Kings' system in 2011, for Carter's old Flyers teammate, Mike Richards.

In 2012, the Kings won the Stanley Cup. They won it again in 2014.

But then Lombardi had a problem on his hands. He had a chance to buy out the rest of Richards' contract, which ran through 2020 at $5.75 million per season, without any cap repercussions. Instead he opted for loyalty: he kept Richards around, because he was a part of two Cup champions, defying any logic when it came to finances or on-ice stats.

The next season, Richards continued to regress. Lombardi eventually put him on waivers and dropped him to the American Hockey League for most of the season. Eventually, he attempted to get out of the contract due to an off-the-ice incident involving Richards in 2015.

Lombardi was aggressive beyond loyalty in acquiring him. He was aggressively blinded by it in keeping him.

But hey, even the best general managers make mistakes. Or else the job really would be "boring as hell."

All of this said…what's the dream team? Both in the front office and on the ice?

Let's say I somehow stumbled into hundreds of millions of dollars—I knew there was a reason I never threw away those Star Wars figures!—and was able to purchase a team. Here's how I'd go about building a franchise.

Team President

Honestly, this has become a public-relations position as much as anything. I'd hire an ex-player with some gravitas—like John Davidson in Columbus and St. Louis, Joe Sakic in Colorado, or what Pat LaFontaine could have been in Buffalo. Someone who can glad-hand ticket holders, but also attract and inspire a coalition of smart hockey people.

General Manager

I'm a big believer in osmosis when it comes to general managers. Guys who have worked within the framework of a successful franchise, although not as the general manager. I like the hunger of an underling, someone who's learned the ropes but wants nothing more than to pilot his own ship in a direction a few degrees away from where his former boss was headed. There's a reason why guys like Jim Nill and Steve Yzerman got their own gigs after having corner offices with the Red Wings.

Philosophically, I want someone who's going to build from the crease out. Defensemen first. The goalie can come from outside the organization; frankly, that's going to be easier than developing one's own. The forwards are the next priority.

And while he's thinking about forwards last, he has to be forward thinking. No dinosaurs. Fully embracing analytics and new tech, fully open-minded to things like sleep studies.

Coach

The coach obviously needs to be tailored to the roster. If it's a young team, I want a coach who can grow with those players until the time comes to fire him and then eventually hire that older, more experienced coach who gets them over the playoff hump. If it's a veteran team, then I need a coach who has some years running the bench to his credit.

Defense wins championships. That's the bottom line. As much as I want to fill the seats with some up-tempo offensive system, I'd likely hire some trap-happy coach whose system can get my team into contention and patch its holes with a conservative style. Boring as that is.

The Roster

Clean slate, full roster to fill? I start on defense, with an emphasis on mobility and puck possession. It's said a goalie can make any team better; well, I think any defense, playing the right system, can make any goalie better. Then I move to center, because NHL success is predicated on what you have up the gut. And because we'll need at least a few goals per game to win. Then the goalie.

Size matters, although I wouldn't be slavish to it. It's a cosmic joke that "undersized" players with dynamic offensive ability aren't given a fair shake because old-school GMs feel like they need battleships instead of motorboats on the roster.

That said, toughness is essential, both on defense and at the forward spot. I don't ascribe to the "enforcer" thing, but you do need one or two players who will go bananas if one of their guys is taken out.

If only it were really that simple.

CHAPTER 11

INSIDE THE DRAFT

One of the greatest rivalries in hockey history occurred off the ice: the National Hockey League vs. the World Hockey Association.

In 1974, the WHA was signing away players who were too young to be drafted by the NHL, which had a 20-year-old minimum for rookies. So the NHL finally responded by dropping the age requirement for the first two rounds of the '74 draft; and to really mess with the WHA, the NHL moved its draft two days before the WHA's in order to have a window of exclusivity to sign selected players.

So paranoid was the NHL that the draft was held via conference call from the league's headquarters in Montreal. This ended up being the wrong choice: the draft selections took so long that it ran the danger of actually overlapping with that of the WHA. It...took...forever.

Buffalo Sabres general manager George "Punch" Imlach was ticked off about how tedious the process was, so he decided to cast one of the most hilarious protest votes in pro sports history.

In the 11th round, with the 183rd pick, Imlach selected Taro Tsujimoto of the Tokyo Katanas in the "Japanese league." Technology being what it was in 1974, there weren't many ways for the NHL to check the credentials on this "star center," according to Imlach. The league rubber-stamped it; rival NHL general managers immediately wondered who this mysterious rookie was.

Weeks later, Imlach came clean. There were no Tokyo Katanas—
"Katana" being Japanese for "sabre"—and there was no Taro Tsujimoto.
Imlach was exasperated by the length of the draft and decided to have a
laugh at its expense. So he made up the pick and submitted it.

The origin of the name was like something out of *The Usual Suspects*,
with Punch as Keyser Söze. One story had Imlach simply picking
Tsujimoto's name out of a phone book; another claimed that Buffalo
owner Seymour Knox III had been served by a waiter with that name
while dining in a Japanese restaurant the evening before the draft.

Whatever the case, the NHL officially refers to that selection in 1974 as
"invalid claim." But the legend continued for years later, as Sabres fans
created Tsujimoto jerseys and one went as far as to create a Tsujimoto
rookie card.

Needless to say, teams today don't draft fictitious players.

Just counterfeit ones.

FOLLOW THE BOUNCING BALLS

The modern NHL draft has no room for such shenanigans. There's
too much information available, too many scouts on the job, too many
eyes on the player pool for any team to draft a completely unknown
commodity. Even if he's from the Tokyo Katanas.

The first NHL draft open to the public was in 1980 in Montreal; the
first one open to the public in the U.S. was in 1987 in Detroit—the
locals witnessed their team take defenseman Yves Racine four spots
ahead of some bum named Joe Sakic.

Beginning in 1995, the NHL instituted a draft lottery that allowed
teams to move up to four positions in the draft order, meaning that the
bottom five teams all had a shot at the first overall pick, although their
chances were weighted.

For the next 10 years, the team with the worst record in the NHL failed to secure the first-overall pick five times.

Its format changed dramatically in 2005, after the NHL deplorably canceled the 2004–05 season due to the lockout. Sidney Crosby was a foundational star player with Rimouski Oceanic of the Quebec Major Junior Hockey League, and a generational talent. The lottery was historic in the sense that it involved all 30 NHL teams. Each team began with three balls in the lottery. For every playoff appearance in the previous three years and every No. 1 overall pick in the draft in the last *four* years, a team lost one ball.

(It also sparked the tradition of having team executives attend the draft lottery in person, like some hockey nerd version of the White House Correspondents Dinner. This leads to that wonderful moment at the start of each broadcast when we see how serious these teams think their chances are. "Oh, you sent Chip the Intern because you have a 0.01 percent chance to win?")

Back in 2005, the Pittsburgh Penguins were among the teams expected to have a strong chance at Crosby.

The Anaheim Ducks were not, given just a 4.16 percent chance of winning the lottery. Yet as the cards were revealed for each team, the Ducks clearly had jumped into the top three. But in the end, it was the Penguins logo that was revealed with the first pick. Delightful Chicago Blackhawks owner Bill Wirtz muttered the word "justice" as then-Canucks GM Brian Burke did the walk of shame back to his chair.

After 2005, the lottery reverted to its previous form until 2015, which featured a lottery that shifted odds away from teams that were at the bottom of the standings in an effort to prevent tanking, and in 2016, when the lottery shifted to a "three mini-lottery" format that selected the first, second, and third picks, with the worst team in the league falling as far as No. 4.

Which is a handy way to avoid tanking but seems counterintuitive to the idea that the draft is supposed to help the weakest teams in the league from being so weak.

AT THE TABLE

It looks like the most chaotic wedding reception imaginable: 30 tables, sprawled out on the floor of an arena, each with about a dozen people seated around it, with a centerpiece that features an NHL team logo. All of them in the shadow of a massive stage with a tote board and a podium, where an impish commissioner will announce selected draft picks and made-on-the-spot trades.

Players are selected from several North American junior hockey leagues, as well as several different European pro leagues. The 2013 NHL Entry Draft was a good representation of this: among the top 10 picks, two were from the Quebec Major Junior League; three were from the Ontario Hockey League; two were from Finland; one was from Sweden; and one was from the decidedly not-amateur Kontinental Hockey League in Russia.

In 2014, 12 different nations made up the 210-player draft pool, including selections from Denmark, Germany, and the U.K.

(The U.S., incidentally, was second overall with 67 players chosen to Canada's 77; as more "non-traditional" markets like California, Texas, Arizona, and Florida start to produce hockey talent, it's not crazy to believe that the Americans could outnumber their neighbors to the north. Next up: we dominate curling!)

In order to suss out which players are worth spending a draft pick on, teams employ a small army of scouts that filter out through the world and track these athletes as many as three years before they're draft eligible. (Players who are 18 on or before September 15 and not older than 20 before December 31 of their draft year are eligible for that year.)

The director of amateur scouting is the point person for all of this, scheduling out where the amateur scouts are headed and attempting to identify players who have exceptional skills or play a role that could fill an organizational need.

"While we're at the table and while we're drafting, we're very cognizant of our depth chart and making sure we continue to fill our depth chart," said senior director of amateur scouting Mark Kelley of the Chicago Blackhawks. "In certain times, we will look at needs on the depth chart, and that really comes down to looking at the value of players; defensemen might have more value because of our depth chart or a forward might have more value because of our depth chart. I guess the simple answer is we're very aware of our organizational depth chart going forward over the next few years."

In Detroit, for the 2014–15 season, the director of amateur scouting had four full-time scouts and three part-timers at his disposal in North America; then there's a director of European scouting who oversees a staff of four Europe-based scouts that covers all of their pro leagues.

The Toronto Maple Leafs went even bigger: 14 amateur scouts and five European scouts, all reporting to the director of amateur scouting.

Everyone then reports to the director of player personnel.

The scouts are tasked with collecting as much information about prospects as they can, through game observations and interviews with teams and other methodology. Then, as the draft approaches, these scouts become advocates or critics for their players. (Keep in mind that evaluation of these players isn't monolithic: even European scouts will travel to give a second or third look at a prospect. There are checks and balances.)

It all culminates in the creation of the NHL draft's most sacred document: the list.

PICKS BY NATIONALITY SINCE 1991

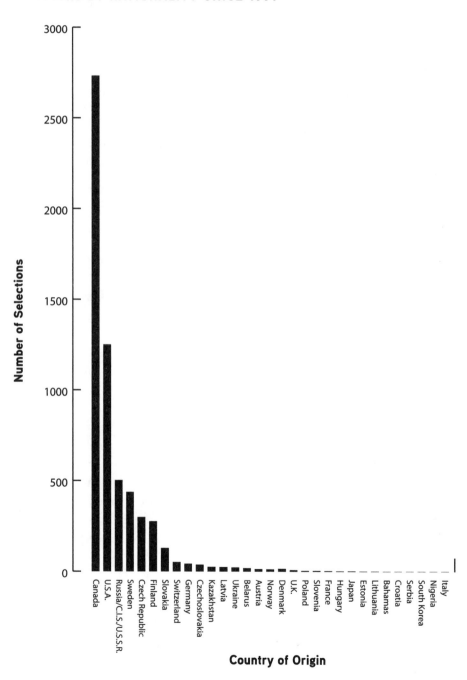

CANADA VS. USA VS. RUSSIA VS. SWEDEN

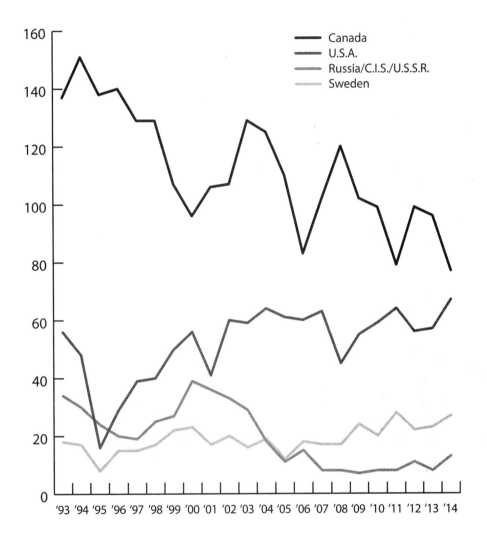

Every team, at every table, comes prepared with a ranking of the players they desire to draft at the draft spots in which they're positioned. Sure, there are always pie-in-the-sky possibilities of players falling down the draft board that they didn't anticipate, but typically the teams know the pool of players who should be there in the first and second rounds.

The general managers step up and get involved in trades on the draft floor, but it's not always their show. Typically, the draft table is run by the director of amateur scouting and the assistant general manager, who have their hands on the player development in the team's minor leagues and have an expert understanding of the organization's needs.

When trades are made to move up or move down, it becomes a poker game: one general manager will contact another, and the guessing begins on whether the team drafting ahead of his will swipe the player he's looking for. Which is why the smart play is to arrive at the table with as many chips as possible: the more lower-round draft choices that a general manager acquires at the trade deadline, the larger his war chest in attempting to move up in the draft.

Sometimes trades are the result of opportunity. The Washington Capitals in 2011 had the No. 26 overall pick. They had been successful in turning lower-round selections into NHL-level prospects in the past, but none of the players they had high on their draft board seemed likely to be there. So GM George McPhee had a conundrum: take a player they liked but didn't love, or see if any teams were interested in swapping a current NHL player for a first-round pick.

He found one with the Chicago Blackhawks, who had a restricted free agent in forward Troy Brouwer, one who had won the Stanley Cup with the team. The Capitals and Blackhawks pulled off the deal, and Washington acquired a versatile forward who became a fan favorite.

"We were more willing to make a deal than in the past at this draft," said McPhee. "We did a lot of mock drafts and did not see that player that we could get in the last few years: top six forward, top four defenseman. We didn't see that kind of difference maker this year. But we knew this player would be available, and he wouldn't be available for long, so we had to move on him."

But while some teams come to the draft to shop for NHL players, the majority are there to select prospects for their future.

THE ROOKIES

Sam Bennett grabbed the bar. His arms flexed, muscles looking like they were going to burst through the skin. He began to raise his torso and his chin moved toward the bar, a feat accomplished in every high-school gymnasium across the country, let alone at the NHL scouting combine.

And then...nothing.

Sam Bennett couldn't do a pull-up.

A projected top-five pick in the 2014 NHL Entry Draft at the time, Bennett's inability to pass that aspect of the fitness test made news around the hockey world. The *Toronto Star* consulted fitness experts' opinions on pull-up deficiency. Others used it as an accusation that Bennett didn't have the proper upper body strength to be a lofty draft choice.

"It really did bother me. It's just...I know I couldn't do them, but obviously I'm going to keep working on them," he said before the draft. "I guess that's how people are labeling me right now. There's nothing I can really do about it, except for work hard in the gym and get better."

He was given phone calls of encouragement from NHL star Jason Spezza, who worked out at his gym, and eventually trained himself to be able to do multiple pull-ups. Bennett was taken at No. 4 overall by the Calgary Flames.

Q: What are the unwritten rules of the NHL Entry Draft?

A: Call them clichés or stereotypes or universal truths, there are certain things you hear every season around NHL draft time. A few of them:

1. Drafting Russians is super risky: For every Alex Ovechkin and Evgeni Malkin, there's a talented Russian player a team passes over because of the politics and headaches involved.

The rise of the Kontinental Hockey League all but killed the late-round Russian prospect, as those players were likely to stay in Russia and play professionally. And teams remain wary of top-level talent, too: Vladimir Tarasenko, a brilliant offensive player, was taken by the St. Louis Blues at No. 16 because teams knew he would spend the first few seasons of his career in Russia. Which he did, jumping to the NHL in 2012 as a 21-year-old after five seasons in the KHL overall.

This perception has greatly affected the number of Russians taken in the draft, from 41 in 2000 to just 13 picks in 2014.

2. Drafting goalies is super risky, too: Unlike your hockey fantasy draft, where the goalies are frequently gobbled up early, the NHL draft finds goalies taken later than skaters. There wasn't a goalie

"What doesn't kill you makes you stronger in the end. To experience this at a young age, maybe helps me get through something when I'm older," he said.

This is one of a hundred examples of NHL prospect hysteria. The coverage of junior, NCAA, and other amateur players has increased exponentially over the years, with NHL prospects under constant scrutiny in their respective leagues and especially on the largest stages: the Memorial Cup, the championship tournament in Canadian junior hockey; the Frozen Four, the NCAA men's hockey tournament; and the taken in the first round of the 2014 draft; Mason McDonald was selected by Calgary at No. 34. In 2013, more of the same: Zach Fucale was taken at No. 36 after no goalies went in the first round. In 2012... well, look at that, the double-whammy: Andrei Vasilevskiy, a Russian goalie taken at No. 19 by the Lightning.

Once in a while, you'll find a can't-miss netminder who will go in the lottery, such as Marc-André Fleury, who went No. 1 overall in 2003. But that's becoming rarer: thanks to advancements in goalie coaching, and the general disregard for the position from some teams eager to just platoon players rather than draft a franchise guy, taking a crack at a raw talent in later rounds is now the trend.

3. The No. 1 pick is not for sale: The last time the first overall pick was traded was in 2003, when the Florida Panthers sent it and a third-round pick to the Pittsburgh Penguins for their No. 3 overall pick, a second-rounder, and Mikael Samuelsson. The Penguins drafted the aforementioned Fleury and the Panthers selected Nathan Horton, who had a nice run with them for nearly a decade.

That completed a wacky five-year run of first overall picks being traded, but it's only happened 10 times since 1971. You earn that No. 1 pick, you keep that No. 1 pick. Unless you're Quebec, in which case you trade that No. 1 pick to two different teams and have a judge finally send Lindros to the Flyers.

International Ice Hockey Federation's Under-20 Championships, or World Juniors for short.

(That latter tournament gives us the annual drama surrounding the Canadian team, whose lack of success can literally spark governmental hearings about the development of youth players, like it's the Soviet Union or something.)

The NHL scouting combine features more than a dozen tests of physical and mental fitness, bringing together the prospects and the NHL teams for some face-to-face time before the draft.

Among the tests:

Body Composition: Measuring a player's percentage of body fat, or, in some cases, baby fat.

Grip Strength: A general test of strength, but a specifically important test for players in a sport where someone is trying to rip the stick out of your grip.

Upper Body Strength: Medicine balls!

Push-ups and Pull-ups: A place where records are set and bragging occurs. Unless you're Sam Bennett.

Long Jump and Vertical Jump: A test of players' leg strength, which is palpable given the sport they play.

Agility Test: Like hopscotch if drawn by MC Escher.

Ergometer: The test that can frequently turn the combine into a vomitorium, as players push their heart rates to 200 beats per minutes in 30-second sprints.

Stationary Bike: Strapping on the mask and testing one's aerobic fitness and breathing.

So yeah, it's super intense.

"The combine fitness segment isn't a competition or a pass-or-fail type of test," NHL director of central scouting Dan Marr told NHL.com. "It allows the NHL strength coaches to see where these players are in their current state of development and identify areas for improvement.

"If you go back 10-15 years, they were more overwhelmed, but now it's impressive how well the players get the support of their junior teams and agents prepare them for this event. This is a genuinely good group of kids. There used to be a time when all these prospects had that deer-in-the-headlights look and were a little apprehensive when they get here. Now they know what's coming because they hear from their friends who have already gone through it. I think the guys in the first testing group are more apprehensive than the others, but once they get going they're just fine."

Do the tests matter?

Not nearly as much as they do in the National Football League, to be honest. Scouts are much more interested in a player's instincts and on-ice performance in hockey, while in football the combine can make or break a player. For Pete's sake, a kid couldn't do a pull-up and still went fourth overall!

What it does is add another layer of data to the compendium written about these prospects, who are known inside and out before they're drafted.

But even that doesn't prevent disaster from striking.

BUSTED!

Ken Daneyko, the rock-solid defenseman who won three Stanley Cups with the New Jersey Devils, tells a story about one of the biggest draft busts in franchise history.

Neil Patrick Brady was a junior hockey star. He scored 81 points in 72 games with the WHL Medicine Hat Tigers in 1985–86. The Devils, looking to add to a collection of great young offensive forwards that included Kirk Muller and John MacLean, drafted him No. 3 overall in the 1986 NHL Entry Draft, ahead of future star Vinny Damphousse and some kid named Brian Leetch.

Q: What happens if a player is drafted and doesn't want to play with that team?

A: Much like free agency, there's a certain element of indentured servitude to the NHL draft. In general, you play where you're drafted, and in general most players are just happy to be drafted by an NHL team.

But once in a while, you have a player who would rather hammer a railroad spike in his ear than suit up for the team that selected him. The teams, in theory, should understand this; but like an unrequited lover in high school, they still think with the right song at prom they can convince their intended otherwise.

That's partially because they own these players' rights for so long. Essentially, a college player's rights are owned through all four years of college or three years as a junior league player (like the USHL). There are loopholes, like the one that Justin Schultz exploited: a player can become a free agent after three years in college if he spent a year playing junior hockey following being drafted.

Otherwise, a player not signed by the team that selected him within two years can reenter the draft, assuming he is still eligible. A "reentry player" is a special category of draftee; he may have escaped a potentially bad situation with the team that drafted him, but he also may have harmed his draft position by reentering it after two seasons.

If he is not eligible, he will become an unrestricted free agent.

The reentry route is rare, seeing as how it means at least two years outside of the NHL development system at a minimum. So the most common remedy to a player who doesn't want to be there?

Trading his rights to somewhere he might want to be.

Granted, not every trade will rise to the epic grandeur of the Eric Lindros debacle with Quebec—perhaps the greatest example of a player opting not to play where he was drafted—but the goal is always to get the team an asset in exchange for an asset it won't otherwise utilize.

"He showed up to camp that year," recalled Daneyko, "and I couldn't believe what I was seeing. This guy, this 18-year-old guy, was getting winded during practice. He was out of shape. And I knew immediately he wasn't going to make an impact for us."

And he didn't. Brady struggled with his confidence in two years in the AHL, and played 29 games with the Devils from 1989 to 1992 before being offered up to the expansion Ottawa Senators for future considerations. He would go on to play 60 more NHL games with Ottawa and Dallas before settling into a seven-year career toiling in the IHL.

Not exactly the stuff of No. 3 overall picks. Consider that 1987's No. 3 was Glen Wesley, a standout defenseman for two decades.

But there have been No. 1 picks that have gone bust, too, and No. 30 picks that have gone on to have star careers. And there have been guys taken in the fifth round who were among the best in the draft, in hindsight. (Hi there, Jamie Benn).

Jamie Bisson of The Score studied the NHL drafts from 2005 to 2010 to find out which rounds give the best value, i.e., deliver NHL players to NHL teams. The findings:

> **Round 1:** 66.7 percent of picks (120 of 180) played at least 100 games in the NHL.

> **Round 2:** 26.7 percent of picks (50 of 187) played at least 100 games.

> **Round 3:** 17.2 percent of picks (31 of 180) played at least 100 games.

> **Round 4:** 14.7 percent of picks (27 of 184) played at least 100 games.

Round 5: 8.6 percent of picks (16 of 187) played at least 100 games.

Round 6: 9.8 percent of picks (18 of 182) played at least 100 games.

Round 7: 7 percent of picks (13 of 186) played at least 100 games.

But if you break it down further, you find that 90.6 percent of first-rounders make at least one appearance in the NHL; that figure drops to 63.1 percent for the second round and 45 percent for the third round. But it's 40.2 percent in the fourth round, telling us that those mid-round picks can produce similar results.

(Not so much the seventh round: only 19.4 percent of the players drafted made the Show, i.e., a less-than-one-in-five chance for success.)

What's more, Scott Cullen of TSN looked back at the picks from 1995 to 2004 and found something striking: the percentage of players taken from Nos. 21-25 in the first round who played more than 100 NHL games was higher (72 percent) than those drafted right outside the top 10, Nos. 11-15 (54 percent).

The number of unknowns and crapshoots taken at the NHL draft far outweigh the number of sure things.

But that's the fun of it: a chance for the great to remain great, the good to get better, and the terrible to sell to fans the only thing that truly does sell in professional sports on an annual basis—hope.

CHAPTER 12

FANCY STATS

Before I entered the University of Maryland as a freshman, I needed to take a math placement test, evaluating my knowledge of the subject and then placing me in a class that reflected that comprehension. I was rather confident that this was a formality, having faked my way through four years of high school math using a combination of copying the odd answers from the back of the book and using chicken scratch to pretend there was an equation that led to that answer, as well as graphing calculator programming skills that would put Mark Zuckerberg to shame.

(And by that of course I mean typing 55378008, flipping it upside down, and seeing BOOBLESS.)

So, with that wind in my sails and a raging head cold, I took the test and did…absolutely terribly. Like, I'm surprised they didn't revoke my admissions letter because I apparently wasn't smart enough to function in life.

I was placed in "Math 001," a class so remedial that I believe the first lesson involved fingers and toes. Now, this would surely shock me into improving myself, right? Surely, this would be the moment in which I recognized my faults and sought to correct them through hard work, tutoring, and intense studies?

Of course…if the class wasn't at 8:00 AM, and I wasn't a freshman studying under the tutelage of Professor Jack Daniels. So I hardly went to class. But when I did, there was a quiz, and I thought to myself, *Oh, how lucky I am to always pick the classes to attend that have quizzes!*

It was some time later that I realized *every* class had a quiz, and that I had failed a substantial portion of them by no-showing.

So I needed a solid grade on the final, lest I fail Math 001 and put my scholarship in jeopardy. I crammed, sweated, tapped previously untapped corners of my mind for numerical knowledge…and earned a C that got me a D in the class and a trip to Math 002 in my second semester.

YES! IN YOUR FACE REMEDIAL COURSE THAT EXPOSED MY HUBRIS!

The point of this biographical digression is to establish that I suck at math. Which isn't always a good thing when your chosen profession is built on a foundation of game stats and salary figures.

While moving up the sportswriting ranks, I'd side-eye baseball's stats and breathe a small sigh of relief that the Bill James–inspired analytics revolution had been confined to a sport full of nerdlingers who use mini-golf pencils to score games and pass down historical stats through the generations like Navajo elders recanting folktales. Hockey favored big, dumb, raw numbers. It was hair metal to baseball's smooth jazz.

Then Jim Corsi came along and helped make hockey just as analytical.

And you know what? Despite my complete lack of mathematic acumen—and, hence, my early intimidation in embracing it—hockey analytics have changed the way I watch, understand, and comprehend hockey, for the better.

As they will for you. Viva las fancy stats!

OF CORSI

In 1998, Jim Corsi was in his sixth year of retirement as a former goaltender. He had 26 games with the 1979–80 Edmonton Oilers, but then spent the majority of his playing days in Italy until calling it a career at age 36 with HC Varese, playing with names like Alessandro Badiani, which sound amazing when you say them with an operatic flourish.

With a background in engineering, Corsi had a job waiting for him in Montreal as a math and science teacher. But he was looking for a post-playing career in hockey. After a few near misses, he found a gig with the Buffalo Sabres: part-time, as goalie coaches were during that era, working with the likes of Dominic Hasek.

But Corsi wasn't content with simply teaching goaltending fundamentals. His background in math made him curious about whether there were hidden truths about the position that went beyond the box score.

One of his theories: a goalie's workload could be better quantified by how many shot *attempts* they faced, rather than simply shots on goal. After all, a goalie like Hasek is flopping around like a trout on a dock after pucks that fly wide of the crease. That's a lot of energy exerted that's not always captured by traditional stats, but could be better evaluated if you counted shots on goal, shots that were missed, and shots that were blocked.

And with that, Jim Corsi invented "Corsi."

Well, OK, he invented the metric that would *become* Corsi; as TSN reporter Bob McKenzie discovered in 2015, it was Oilers blogger Tim Barnes, aka Vic Ferrari, who heard Sabres GM Darcy Regier discussing the stat on the radio and decided to name it Corsi, because he thought it sounded better than "Regier." (The hockey world is forever indebted to him for that.)

Related tangent: did you know how invisible braces were invented?

Dental equipment companies worked in conjunction with NASA's Advanced Ceramics Research program to create transparent tooth aligners, helping to replace those steel girders that acted as kissing repellent for decades. The materials were actually made from transparent polycrystaline alumina, which was invented for use in aeronautics for missiles and rockets.

The point is that one person's transparent polycrystaline alumina for use in heat-seeking missiles is another person's invisible braces. The intentions of one are repurposed by the enterprising thoughts of another.

Which is what happened to Jim Corsi's analytics once bloggers got their Cheetos-dusted mitts on them.

The post-2005 lockout era was a boom time for hockey blogging. New platforms gave rise to new voices, and these members of an alternative hockey media were slowly being embraced by teams that were suddenly climbing out of the abyss of obscurity after a lost season. Some of the coverage featured candid opinions about the team, some of it was armchair journalism, and some of it was just pages of Sidney Crosby with a pacifier Photoshopped in his mouth. Hey, to each his own.

But there was one growing subset in blogging that really blazed a trail: the analytics community.

They rose to prominence as a check-and-balance on lazy narratives: the ones established through analysis of traditional stats, but more to the point the ones established by traditional media. Old-school scribes bristled at the criticism, waylaying the bloggers with the tired "mom's basement in their underwear" retorts, only this subset of the genre was actually comprised of lawyers and engineers making roughly five times what the reporters were.

It was that community that took Corsi and repurposed it as a way to measure puck possession: if a goalie is facing more scoring chances than his counterpart, then the opposition likely has possession of the puck longer than that goalie's team does.

If a player's Corsi percentage is above 50 percent, he's considered a positive possession player. Let's say Anze Kopitar is on the ice for 18 shot attempts for his team—not necessarily taken by him—and six against. That's a Corsi-For percentage of 75 percent. That's pretty damn great, and Kopitar would be rightfully lauded as one of the best two-way players in the game.

So Corsi became a catchall proxy for possession; soon it branched out into measuring how teams possessed the puck in certain scoring situations (like if the score was "close") and how players rated against their teammates, depending on what happened to team Corsi when they were on the ice, off the ice, or playing with different linemates or defensive partners.

But rather than being the only standard, Corsi sparked a revolution that led to other metrics.

Matt Fenwick never fancied himself as a member of the analytics elite, but the Calgary Flames blogger and electrical engineer had a question about Corsi's effectiveness: would it be more accurate if blocked shots were removed? His justification, as he wrote in 2007:

"A shot that is blocked is either a) not a scoring chance at all, or b) on average from a worse scoring area than shots/posts/missed shots. Yes it affects the 'sample size' but that only means anything if what you are sampling is relevant to what you are trying to represent."

And with that, Matt Fenwick invented "Fenwick."

In the long run, Fenwick is more predictive than Corsi when it comes to scoring, but its drawback is sample size: the long run is, in fact,

» HOCKEY'S BIGGEST GARBAGE STATS

This is a chapter about stats that have value. Let's talk about a few that...don't.

Plus-Minus: There are times when analytics feel like a direct response to this rice-paper-thin evaluation of a player's value. For decades, players were defined by how many goals for and against occurred when they were on the ice at even strength. Which meant that a player could be 200 feet away from a goal being scored, picking his nose while whistling "Brass Bonanza," having affected the play as much as you or I had, and he received a plus or a minus. Yes, when you have extremes like a plus-30 or a minus-30, something can be gleaned from it. But being a slightly minus player tells us nothing... unless you want to yank back Nicklas Lidstrom's 2011 Norris Trophy when he was (GASP!) a minus-1.

Secondary Assists: Speaking of getting praise for doing essentially nothing. As analytics blogger Neil Greenberg said: "The secondary assist is overvalued. There are so many instances where a player touches the puck and it eventually gets into the net, but there's no evidence that the touch did anything to affect that play. And yet the player gets an assist."

Turnovers: One of the most misunderstood and misappropriated stats in hockey. Take a player like Erik Karlsson of the Ottawa Senators, who led the NHL in turnovers in 2013–14 and is frequently among the league leaders in

thousands of shots, which take longer to tabulate when you take blocked shots out of the mix.

For years, analytics bloggers would use these stats as an antidote for vapid analysis of the game. Eventually, it became apparent that their research was running parallel to that of NHL teams.

"If you asked 30 coaches how important puck possession was, they'd all say very important. If you asked them how important Corsi was, they'd look at you like you had three heads," said Neil Greenberg, an analytics writer for the *Washington Post*. "But we were always speaking the same language."

giveaways. Does he make mistakes? Of course. But that's not the catalyst for his turnovers. Constantly having the puck on his stick, having the Senators' offense run through him, and having more ice time than any other defenseman in the league save for Ryan Suter...those are the catalysts. And they don't point to Karlsson being a weak-wristed turnover machine, or *else they wouldn't give him the puck so damn much.*

To that end: No. 2 in turnovers in 2014–15 was John Tavares of the New York Islanders, with 109, and he was nominated for the Hart Trophy.

Faceoffs: Not *totally* a garbage stat. Faceoffs are important. Faceoffs lead to puck possession. Winning them in certain situations, like in the defensive zone on a penalty kill, is pretty vital.

The problem with faceoffs is that we don't know enough about them. Sometimes players lose them on purpose. So do you categorize that as a win or a loss? I mean, if the player's job is to lose, and he loses, isn't that a win?

But more than anything, faceoffs lack that "next level" of context that could make them much more revelatory. "I would like to see adjusted faceoff percentage," said Greenberg. "If I take a faceoff against Jonathan Toews, and I lose, well, it's Jonathan Toews. We know how good he is. It would be much more interesting to see how well he does against other top-flight faceoff guys. Like an adjusted strength of schedule thing."

Now that's valuable.

Like any counter-culture movement, Corsi and Fenwick eventually became mainstream. The NHL added possession stats to its website in 2015, but went all "Don Draper at the hippie commune" and renamed them "blocked and unblocked shot attempts," sucking the uniqueness from them and attempting to send Corsi to the same nostalgic trash heap as the Prince of Wales Conference and the Norris Division.

But the analytics community didn't embrace the change, opting for the legacy names when discussing the possession stats—and, over time, discovering their limitations.

"Corsi gives us a decent proxy of puck possession at the team level and at the individual level. But there's still so much we don't know," said Greenberg. "It's still way better than, say, plus-minus, but it doesn't tell us why stuff is happening. It tells us this player and this player are playing well together, but it doesn't tell us why they do. It's pretty clear that Corsi is a rudimentary gauge because there are so many unknowns that go into that variable."

HOW TO EVALUATE A SKATER

As in-depth as hockey stats have become, comparing them to those utilized in baseball and basketball can sometimes be like comparing a pencil sketch to a Rembrandt.

In baseball, technology has advanced to the point where every pitch can be broken down into a dozen variables, with each hitter's tendencies for pitch location, speed, and game situation getting categorized and archived.

In basketball, we know how many points a player scores per minute of play, but also how they score them: How many were scored in transition? How many were jumpers? How many were drives to the net? And on drives to the net, did the player go left or right? And after they went left or right, was the end result a layup or a dunk? And who was defending the player?

Compare that with hockey, for the moment: we know where a shot was generated, and whether it was a wrist shot or a slap shot. We'll soon know its speed. But there's no quantifying the incidents that led to the shot. There's no pinpointing how it beat a goalie. There's no clear picture of how that player was defended on the play.

So we all make our best guesses when evaluating skaters. And thanks to fancy stats, those guesses can be accurate and insightful.

A good starting point for player evaluation is usage. That's what sets expectations for how a player should perform.

Zone starts explain where a player begins and ends his shift. Generally, you'll see an even split amongst the defensive, offensive, and neutral zones, but occasionally you'll see fluctuations: for example, a young offensive defenseman being protected by his coach by getting a disproportionate number of shifts starting in the offensive zone rather than his own, as Torey Krug was with the Boston Bruins as a rookie.

After establishing where the player is, it's time to figure out with whom he's playing. That's where quality of teammates comes in. On its surface, it's pretty obvious: playing with talented players will lead to more success on the ice, while playing with fourth-line grinders will not. But it's a little harder to evaluate than that. For example, let's say you have players who play every shift with Sidney Crosby, but never against Sidney Crosby. It would be difficult to tease apart which one of those players is, say, the better possession player. Although the default answer is usually "Sidney Crosby is better."

"We don't know if a guy like Nicklas Backstrom is successful because he's playing with Alex Ovechkin or if it's because his passes are more accurate than others. We don't know how he rates against others in the NHL if they were in his situation," said Greenberg.

That said, you can see variations in Corsi percentage for players when they're with certain teammates relative to others. This is especially true for defensive pairings, where a player's on-ice possession numbers can increase if he's paired with a Corsi machine and decrease if he's paired with a totem pole on skates. This is otherwise known as Relative Corsi, which measures how a player drives possession relative to the rest of the team.

Next comes quality of competition, which is a bit trickier. "QualComp" measures the average on/off-ice plus-minus of opposing players faced by a player. "Corsi Rel Quality of Competition" is a popular measure of a player's effectiveness, as it's the average Relative Corsi of opposing players that's weighted by their time on ice.

Caveat: the "quality" of competition has much to do with whom your opponents are facing throughout the season, and what kinds of players those lines are playing against. For example, a matchup between two top lines might not actually feature the two best possession lines. It could be that the second line is actually seeing the "tougher" competition, and the numbers aren't always going to reflect that.

Now that we've established where players are, whom they're playing with, and who they're playing against, we can begin to evaluate what exactly they're doing with the puck.

SCORING THE SCORING CHANCES

Zone entries are a facet of analytics that has gotten much attention, particularly as an argument against the classic "dump and chase" method of hockey. At the 2013 Sloan Sports Conference, authors Eric Tulsky, Geoffrey Detweiler, Robert Spencer, and Corey Sznajder presented evidence that showed carrying the puck over the blue line generated roughly twice as many scoring chances as dumping and chasing it.

But zone entries also have a direct effect on possession numbers. And by that I mean those stats can totally shift the blame for a player's apparent inability to possess the puck to a coach who isn't allowing him to do so.

"It added another dimension of detail to Corsi. If this person is driving play, that's great—but how are they driving play? Are they good at carrying the puck into the zone often? Are they playing with someone who does? Are they hamstrung because they're asked to dump the puck in because the system says they do? All these things factor into it," said Greenberg.

» CONTEXT IS KING

Before we even think of evaluating a player, know this: analysis is only as good as the data it's based on. While player-tracking technology—chips placed on players and the puck, and infrared cameras collecting real-time data—will make stats more in-depth and uniform, the data you see on leading stats sites is scraped from play-by-play sheets and box scores being kept by flawed, neurotic human beings in the press box of every arena.

The same ones who spend their time during games determining what, exactly, counts as a "hit."

But, hey, it's the best we have right now. As Bruce Springsteen once sang, "You ain't a beauty, but hey, you're alright. That's alright with me."

What helps lessen the human impact are averages. Rather than raw numbers, the best evaluation of players are averages for goals, assists, points, and shot attempts per 60 minutes. Sample sizes for things like shooting percentage and save percentage have to be large enough to weed out the flukes and anomalies.

Another consideration: game situations.

Most stats sites are going to allow you to evaluate teams and players based on different game situations (even strength vs. the power play) and scoring situations (if the score is tied, close, or if the game's a blowout). Generally, five-on-five stats are what's used to evaluate a player, but always keep in mind things like "score effects," i.e., if a team's possession numbers fall off a cliff in the third period because they're leading in a blowout and hanging back while the other team attacks.

From quality of teammates and opponents to the score and time of the game, there's plenty more to the story that advanced stats tell.

Once players are in the zone, how do we measure their scoring chances? As technology improves, we'll finally get that sense of location and speed of a shot. We already have designations of "high danger" or "low danger" chances, as well.

"Those tell me more about the defense," said Greenberg. "If a goalie has a strong season, a defense in front of him could be way improved, cutting down the high-danger chances."

Let's say our skater scores a goal. And then another. And then two more in the next game. And then, in a two-month span, 14 in total.

Hot streak! Wearing the funny player of the game hat in the locker room! Time for that contract extension!

Well, no, not really. Because analytics have provided needles for these balloons, putting lucky streaks in context.

"PDO" is the sum of a team's on-ice shooting percentage and a team's on-ice save percentage. It helps establish which teams are playing over their heads at even strength and will eventually regress to the mean. As blogger turned Leafs front office consultant Cam Charron puts it, "'Regression' here is the theory that since every shot taken in the NHL must result in a save or a shot, the mean PDO in the NHL is 1. The longer a player or team plays, the closer its PDO will get to 1."

So anything above or below 1.00 can be seen as good luck or bad luck. Although some players always trend above or below it.

For an individual, shooting percentage is still the most basic way to track those fluctuations. It's all about sample size: if our hot-streaker has a shooting percentage at Ovechkin levels when he's typically been Daniel Winnik over a three-year span, chances are he's going to regress.

So, like, burn that contract extension. Burn it with fire.

As with most fancy stats, these anomalies can be explained away. But not all performances are predictive.

"The analytics community is very good at targeting in on extremes. If you have a team that's been very lucky in high shooting percentage or save percentage, the analytics are very good in saying this is or isn't sustainable. But that's only about 20 percent of the league," said Greenberg. "The rest of the 80 percent, it's difficult to say if someone's going to have a breakout season after having average numbers. What makes that person go from a 10-goal season to a 20-goal season? I haven't seen a dependable way to predict that."

Perhaps it depends on the goalies they're facing…

GETTING DEEP IN THE CREASE

If it's flying in the air, Chris Boyle is probably trying to catch it.

Boyle, an analytics blogger who's worked with Sportsnet, was a baseball catcher for 15 years and played goalie during his spare time. He appreciates both positions, but laments that the value of a catcher is easier to ascertain through analytics than that of a hockey goalie.

"The new data they have in baseball can tell you that catchers are worth six wins more a year just based on their pitch framing. That's not even taking into account their knowledge of how to pitch to players," he said.

Goalie analytics don't have the widespread acceptance of those for skaters. Part of this is due to the fact that the data available for players trying to keep the puck out is so narrow and miniscule compared to the stats kept for those trying to put the puck in the net. Goalies have wins, goals-against average, and save percentage, the latter two parsed for different game situations.

» BRIEF GUIDE TO FANCY STATS

Here are some of the hockey analytics every fan should know:

Corsi: Named in honor of former NHL goalie Jim Corsi, it's the sum of shots on goal, shots that are blocked, and shots that missed the net. The most common measure of puck possession at even strength. Corsi-For percentage is Corsi-For divided by Corsi-For plus Corsi-Against.

Corsi Rel: As War On Ice puts it, Corsi Rel is "the player's on-ice Corsi percentage minus the player's off-ice Corsi percentage; off-ice Corsi percentage is the percent of shot attempts taken by the player's team when the player is not on the ice (but in games where the player is in the lineup)." Translated: a handy way to compare the possession numbers between players.

Fenwick: Named for blogger Matt Fenwick, the other most common measure of puck possession. It's the sum of shots on goal and shots that miss the net, but not blocked shots.

PDO: The sum of even-strength shooting percentage and even-strength save percentage. Essentially, it's a measurement of luck. The mean is typically 1.00; some players are constantly above that, but some regress to that mean after hot streaks. Conversely, some linger below it.

Quality of Competition: As Behind the Net puts it, the "average Relative Plus-Minus of opposing players, weighted by head-to-head ice time." But the stat has expanded over the years to focus on Corsi, giving a better idea of the possession stats for opponents in comparison to your own player.

Quality of Teammates: The average relative plus-minus of players, based on how much time they shared on the ice. Like quality of competition, this has been expanded to Corsi as well. Typically, statheads prefer "with or without you" (WOWY) numbers that compare two linemates' possession numbers.

Zone Starts: Where a player begins and ends his shifts in one of the three zones on the ice. An essential way to figure out if some players are being better positioned to succeed than others—or protected.

"Even-strength save percentage would be the best metric available, but even then you're not really separating much. It's pretty basic. It's just the next generation: you had wins, you had goals-against average, and now you have save percentage," said Boyle.

But even as an elementary stat, by comparison, save percentage can at the very least separate the stars from the suck.

"Good goalies don't give you an .896 save percentage. Ever. You can weed out bad, but you can't separate good from great," he said.

Boyle and other goalie-stats gurus have dedicated their time to opening up the analytics behind a netminder's performance, both in the short and the long term. Their focus is less about the pucks that fly over the goal line and more about all of the events leading up to a goal.

A good sample size for a goalie? Boyle says 3,000 shots faced. "We've seen goalies go on a run of 1,000 shots and look unbeatable. But at 3,000, you're going to see a little bit of that reality creep in," he said.

But what do those shots look like?

Boyle tracked 33,535 shots on goal in the NHL. He found that 28,398 of them were "clean": your typical untouched slapper or wrister inside the offensive zone. Of those, 1,388 ended up in the net.

He found 2,234 of them were in transition. He found 1,640 of them were off rebounds. He found that 1,263 of them came on deflections.

Here's the rub: of those other types of shots on goal, Boyle found 1,412 goals were scored. "Half the goals in the league, on 10 percent of the shots, are scored on high-end chances: pre-shot passes, deflections, rebounds," he said.

What that means is that teams adept at preventing those types of shots are generally going to have dominant goaltending. The Boston Bruins under Claude Julien were one such team: Tim Thomas and Tuukka

Rask both won Vezina Trophies playing behind a defense that limited the scoring chances to low-percentage shots. And playing behind a sequoia that took human form named "Zdeno."

Steve Valiquette, the former backup goalie for the New York Rangers, developed his own advanced goalie stats as well, breaking down goals into two categories. There are "Green Goals," ones that are scored off high-percentage shots like one-timers, deflections, screens, and rebounds; low-percentage shots are called "Red Goals." Through the first three months of the 2014–15 season, 76 percent of the goals scored were Green Goals.

What Boyle looks for in shot quality is how much real estate a goalie has to cover in making a save. "The pass coming across, the goalie trying to transition, all that lateral movement," he said.

What he hopes for in the future is technology that can better track that movement in the crease. "When you see a goalie skate from spot to spot, there's efficiency there. There needs to be a way to track that movement," said Boyle. "It's not really different than when you see the Raptors say that LeBron James is a perfect defender, always where he's supposed to be. That would show up for the truly great goalies."

So like so many other statheads, Boyle waits for the technology to catch up to his wants and needs for data, specifically on shot attempts.

"We have no velocity tracking. Some rebounds are right in front of you, and the second shot is pretty easy to save. There's a ton of extra layers that need to be added to the metric," he said. "The two that would be the most important are velocity and pre-shot movement. How much time a goaltender has to set himself before a shot. There are knuckleballs, and then there are Ovechkin shots."

Yes, Ovechkin shots. Scud missiles fired from the circle, laser guided to the top corner of the net over a goalie's blocker side.

"Everyone knows there are certain plays on which the goalie doesn't have a chance. Certain plays where it doesn't matter what the goalie does," said Boyle. "The best goalies are the ones who stop the shots they're supposed to."

FANCY STATS VS. EYE TESTS

On October 29, 2013, *Toronto Sun* columnist Steve Simmons cracked his knuckles, placed his fingers on his keyboard, and tweeted.

He tweeted with purpose: the Toronto Maple Leafs were 9–4–0, and had scored 44 goals to 30 surrendered. Reports of their demise were widespread, as their possession numbers in the previous season were atrocious, their team shooting percentage was a bubble ready to burst, and the systems of coach Randy Carlyle seemed doom to fail despite a playoff berth in the previous season.

But the Leafs were off to a good start. In, you know, *October.*

Simmons was a sworn enemy of the hockey stats community, an avowed analytics atheist in a time of enlightenment. So he gloatingly tweeted, "Good thing the Leafs don't play in the CHL. The CORSI hockey league. They're doing just fine in NHL, though."

The Leafs finished 38–36–8. They gave up 256 goals and scored just 231. They finished last in the NHL in Corsi percentage, at 44.1. And, we assume, last in the Corsi Hockey League, as well.

Another battle was in the books between the "go beyond the box score" evolutionists and the "shut up and watch the games" traditionalists. A war with significant casualties. And by that we mean people blocking each other on Twitter.

Oh, the humanity.

Brian Burke is as old school as they come, from the decades at the rinks to the unfastened necktie to the hair that makes him look like a middle-aged Sonic the Hedgehog.

"I think it's still an eyeballs business," Burke said in 2014, at Sloan. "We go watch players play. We watch for a lot of things in games that even video won't show. How players respond when a coach yells at them. If they're on the ice and they make a bad play and allow a goal to happen, their body English. How they rally their teammates. Things like that."

The Calgary Flames president once added this bit of color: "Stats are like a lamppost to a drunk. Useful for support but not illumination."

But as stats continue to evolve, so does the rivalry between schools new and old. Even Burke's open-minded about it.

"I think people confuse statistics and arithmetic and mathematics with analytics. Analytics to me are, can you take data and do some predictive work that will help me draft or trade better?" he said in 2014. "I haven't seen a system that comes close to doing that. Statistical analysis about faceoffs and where guys play, we use that all the time. We've been using it for 20 years. To me, that's not analytics. Anyone here that has a system worth buying, we pay cash."

And teams *have* paid cash. Analytics bloggers have been gobbled up by teams, like Tyler Dellow with the Edmonton Oilers and Darryl Metcalf, founder of stats site ExtraSkater.com, with the Maple Leafs. Mathematicians, engineers, poker aces…they're all finding work in the NHL in positions created for their analytic insight, working with executives who still believe in nebulous concepts like "grit" that send stats guys into sarcastic giggles.

But even with that divide, there's now a mutual respect between the two extremes.

"I'll go to former players or scouts and say, 'Here's what the numbers are telling me, and you need to tell me what you see out there.' I'm going back to the eye test, which a lot of analytics people railed against in the past," said Greenberg. "Not because it wasn't valuable, but because it didn't tell us everything. And yet now, the high-level metrics don't tell us everything either."

But they do tell us more than we ever previously knew through traditional stats. Which has opened up the game in ways we never anticipated. Even for those of us who need an abacas to figure out a waiter's gratuity.

CHAPTER 13

THE HOCKEY GLOSSARY

Hockey can be a little intimidating for newbie fans. Lots of odd traditions, lots of odd rules. Complicating matters: lots of odd jargon that can sometimes make the game seem impenetrable.

Yet it's anything but! You just have to know your dusters from your grinders and your apples from your sauce…

Here's a hockey glossary so you can refresh your hockey brain or learn the colloquial vocabulary for the first time.

Active Stick: When a player uses his stick for strong defensive play. Although sometimes your stick can be too active, and that's when you get yourself in trouble. Such is in hockey as it is in life.

Alternate Captain: Do not call them assistant captains. DO NOT.

Apple: Alternate name for assists, created by Canadians who figured hockey just isn't folksy enough.

Art Ross Trophy: Given to the player who amasses the most points in a season. Wayne Gretzky won the Art Ross 10 times: seven times with Edmonton, and three more after he was included in the Jimmy Carson Trade with Los Angeles.

Babysitter: A star player used on a line with two less-than-stellar players in order to boost their numbers.

Bag Skate: Torturous practice initiated by a coach to send a message to his players after a difficult stretch or a bad loss. So called because players are "skating their bags off." Bags in this case meaning…well, you get the picture.

Bar Down: When a shot hits the crossbar and then crosses the goal line. Usually after a player tries to go top shelf.

Barn: A hockey rink or hockey arena. Also infamously where Brian Burke and Kevin Lowe, two adult male hockey executives, were once going to fight over the latter's signing of free agent Dustin Penner from the former. Like, with their fists. Did we mention "adult executives"?

Beauty: A compliment of the highest order to a teammate, who might not be good at hockey but makes the locker room laugh and undoubtedly has the most embarrassing yarns to spin.

Bender: A terrible skater whose legs bend inward because he can't keep them straight. Also, what he'll inevitably go on after being abused by his opponents.

Black Aces: A "team within a team" composed of healthy scratches and players returning from injury that travels with the team.

Biscuit: Another name for the puck. A nice bit of symmetry for when your great aunt's charred biscuits are compared to hockey pucks.

Boarding: When a player checks or pushes a defenseless opponent into the boards, causing a violent collision with said boards. Can be a minor or major penalty depending on the severity of the hit.

#BucciOvertimeChallenge: Inspired by ESPN friend of hockey John Buccigross, this becomes a trending topic on Twitter whenever a game heads to overtime. You pick one potential OT hero from each team; winners receive a commemorative shirt, the grandest of grand prizes!

Bucket: Another name for a helmet. Players are known to "flip their buckets" before a fight.

Butt-Ending: When a player uses the shaft of the stick, above the upper hand, to check an opponent. And by check we mean "hit in the mouth." It's a double minor for an attempted one, and a major for a successful one.

Butterfly: A style of goaltending in which a netminder drops to his knees to cover the lower part of the net. Contrary to popular belief, it's not named in honor of the tedious defensive cocoon their teams go into in front of them.

Calder Trophy: Given by the Professional Hockey Writers Association to the player selected as the most proficient in his first year of competition in the NHL, provided he's under the age of 26 and overhyped by the media all season.

Celly: Slang for celebration, as in "Sick celly, bro." The kind of hockey slang that makes it sound like you're trying too hard.

Charging: Penalty based on how far a player travels to deliver a check, especially a jumping one, it may result in a minor, major, or game misconduct penalty. Like roughing, a penalty that's arbitrarily assessed more often than not.

Cherry Picking: When a player hangs at the edge of the defensive zone or the neutral zone, waiting for an outlet pass. He's usually well rested, not having spent any of his precious energy assisting his teammates on defense.

Chiclets: Teeth that have fallen out of one's mouth by force, ironically making it harder for a player to chew Chiclets.

Clipping: Just like in the NFL, a hit below the knees. Unlike the NFL, the player falling doesn't weigh 350 pounds.

Chirp: Hockey parlance for taunting. Wives and kids are usually off limits. Usually.

Clarence Campbell Bowl: The award given to the Western Conference champion, which was formerly given to the Campbell Conference champion before the NHL changed the names of all the conferences and divisions because they think American fans are idiots.

Dangle: A sick stick-handling move by a scorer, filled with dekes and toe drags and other moves designed to embarrass a defender. Also, "stick-handling" and "sick dangle" are just great bedfellows. (See also: "Hockey Porn.")

Corsi: Named for popular former goalie Jim Corsi, it measures puck possession. It's all shot attempts that were on goal, blocked, or missed the net.

Dashers: Another name for the boards, which are made with rigid metal frames. It more specifically refers to the lower part of the boards where the puck—wait for it—"dashes" along when shot around the rink.

Deke: A move a skater uses to fake out a defender and/or a goalie. (True story: a college dorm mate made me cry with anger by using the deke move on Sega's *NHLPA Hockey '93* to win 10–0, and then subsequently threatened me with a butter knife when I complained.)

Don Cherry: The legendary former NHL coach whose commentaries on *Hockey Night in Canada* were as unsettling to many viewers (Europeans and women among them) as the patterns on his jackets were unsettling to those with functioning retinas.

Dots Down: The area from the faceoff dots in the defensive or attacking zones down to the goal line.

Dump and Chase: When on the forecheck, a team fires the puck to the corner and then tries to retrieve it. What your coach is telegraphing when he says the team needs to "get back to basics."

Duster: Label used to mock a player who rides the bench, i.e., "collecting dust." Also used to describe the magnificent facial hair that appears on players during "Movember" and/or Lanny McDonald.

Elbowing: The use of an extended elbow in a manner that might or might not cause injury. It may result in a minor, major, or game misconduct penalty. Also, my favorite kind of macaroni.

Face Wash: When a player takes his wet, smelly glove and rubs it over the face of an opposing player. It's gross and indignant.

Fighting Strap: A piece of fabric built into the back of a jersey that loops around a player's belt and prevents the jersey from being pulled over his head. If it's not attached and a player's gear comes flying off in a fight, he gets a game misconduct. The rule was inspired by former Buffalo Sabres pugilist Rob Ray, whose jersey and shoulder pads quickly dropped off during fights.

Five-Hole: The gap between the goalie's legs. The one-hole is bottom left and then it moves counter clockwise to the four-hole at top left. Not the weakest spot in a goalie's game, however, thanks to their insatiable dedication to cheating.

Fenwick: A stat that measures puck possession, it's shots on goal plus all shot attempts that missed the net but not ones that were blocked.

Flow: Slang for a player's long hair. Sample prose: "Jaromir Jagr had the sickest flow as a rookie because his hair looked like someone laid out a hundred yak pelts on an airport runway."

Freezing the Puck: Forcibly stopping the momentum of the puck in order to get a stoppage in play, such as when a goalie covers it or a player traps it along the boards with a skate. Not to be confused with icing.

Gagarin Cup: The Stanley Cup of the Russian Kontinental Hockey League, it's the only trophy in professional sports to be named in honor of a cosmonaut.

Garbage Goal: An ugly goal scored that has no right being scored. This is what you get on a funky bounce or a goalie sleeping on the play.

Gong Show: A game that descends into chaos, with fights and penalties and zero defense.

Gordie Howe Hat Trick: When one player scores a goal, assists on another, and engages in a fight during the same game. Ironically, Howe himself only had two Gordie Howe Hat Tricks in his career.

Greasy: Typically applied to a goal scored from a high-traffic area that isn't a thing of beauty, or a player who scores that type of goal, or often the consistency of his hair.

Grinder: A player defined by his hard work on the forecheck and in the corners, without the cumbersome burden of offensive expectations. Also what a sub sandwich is called in misguided parts of the U.S.

Gretzky's Office: The area directly behind the goal cage where the Great One would set up plays in the offensive zone and where modern players make terrible passes trying to emulate him.

Grocery Stick: One of the greatest bits of hockey lingo—a useless player who rides the bench and separates the lines or the forwards from the defense, like a stick at the grocery store checkout separating one customer's items from another's.

Hand Pass: Using one's glove to make a pass to a teammate. It's legal in the defensive zone, not so much elsewhere.

Hart Trophy: Given by the Professional Hockey Writers Association to the player "judged most valuable to his team." It should be awarded to a goalie every season, but it's nice that they let the skaters think they're as important despite playing a third of the time.

Hash Marks: Two parallel lines located on either side of each faceoff dot. Players remain on their side of the hash mark, nearest to their goal, until the puck is dropped. Unless they cheat and the linesman doesn't see them.

Healthy Scratch: When a coach decides a player completely capable of playing in a game will not play in a game. Sometimes because there's no room in the lineup. Sometimes because the coach wants to send a message about the poor quality of the player's performances. The best news of all? Scratched players frequently sit in the press box near people like me, and I'm super fun to sit near.

High-Sticking: When a player's stick makes contact with an opponent above the shoulders, resulting in a minor (incidental contact) or a double-minor (contact that causes an injury) or a match penalty (basically trying to see if candy will fall out of an opponent's head if it's whacked hard enough).

Hip Check: A check delivered with the hip first that's usually designed to flip an opposing player in the middle of the ice. Delivered perfectly, it's a work of dangerous art. Delivered poorly, and it's a cheap shot at the knees of an opponent.

Hockey Porn: A burgeoning fan tradition on social media, this refers to the seemingly unending stream of hockey terms that, stripped of context, sound aggressively pornographic. Lots of sticks. Lots of holes. Lots of sliding. You get the point.

"Hockey Song, The": The seminal classic by Stompin' Tom Connors that's either your favorite sing-along or a catalyst for cynical sighing. Still, though: "They storm the crease/Like bumblebees" is poetry.

Holding: Any action by a player that restrains or impedes the progress of an opposing player whether or not he is in possession of the puck. But let's be honest: it's when one player either bear hugs another or yanks his jersey in a visible manner.

Hooking: Using the stick in a manner that enables a player to restrain an opponent.

Icing: When a player in possession of the puck shoots it across the red line, the opposing team's blue line and goal line, and it isn't touched by an opposing player and doesn't go into the net. In the NHL, the opposing player used to have to touch the puck after that sequence to earn a whistle; but seeing as how broken bodies are bad for business, the league has adopted "hybrid icing," in which the linesman stops play if it's clear the defending player would have gotten to the puck first. After an icing, the puck comes down to the other end for a faceoff, and the team that iced the puck can't make a change. There is no icing for teams playing shorthanded.

Inside the Glass: The position between the benches where television announcers like Pierre McGuire of NBC are situated, giving viewers a real inside look at the game that really should capture more of the obscenities being tossed around down there.

Instigator Rule: A controversial rule implemented in 1992 that penalized a player determined to have started a fight. (Controversial in that it seemed to protect rats and punish enforcers.) An instigator is hit with a minor penalty, a major penalty, and a 10-minute misconduct. If that player is also the "aggressor" in a fight, he gets a game misconduct. If a player gets one in the final five minutes of regulation, he's also suspended for a game. If a player gets three instigator penalties in the same season, it's a two-game suspension; for four, it's four games; for five, it's six games.

Intent to Blow: An actual thing where the referee ends a play *in his mind* before anyone hears him blow the whistle. In a sport where every young player is told to "play to the whistle," mind you.

Interference: Basically any physical impediment of a player who doesn't have the puck. It's a nebulous, inconsistently called minor penalty (usually, although majors can be called) until scoring levels around the NHL drop due to tight defense, and then it's called pretty much every seven minutes.

Jack Adams Award: Given by the NHL Broadcasters Association to the coach "adjudged to have contributed the most to his team's success." He usually meets one of three criteria: a coach who turned a terrible non-playoff team into a playoff team, especially in his first year; a coach who was hired during the season and turned the team's season around; or the coach of the best team in the league.

Jersey Foul: When fans put something other than a player's name and number on the back of their sweaters. There are many exceptions that will allow for some creativity on jerseys; anything involving the number 69 likely does not reach those standards.

Line Brawl: A huge fight involving most of the players on the ice, and frequently the goalies. Before the NHL's crackdown on the practice, this would then lead to a benches-clearing brawl.

Mario Lemieux Hat Trick: Like Mario, it's better than the average hat trick. Named for the cycle of five goals Lemieux scored in December 1988 against the New Jersey Devils: he scored on a power play, shorthanded, at even strength, on a penalty shot, and on an empty net. It's a feat unmatched in NHL history.

Mark Messier Leadership Award: An award invented in 2006 to attract sponsorship and serve its namesake's ego, it honors players who "lead by positive example through on-ice performance, motivation of team members, and a dedication to community activities and charitable causes."

Murphy Dump: Coined by Penguins announcer Mike Lange, it's a clearing attempt in which the puck is flipped over the heads of everyone out of the zone. Named for Hall of Fame defenseman Larry Murphy.

Masterton Trophy: Given by the Professional Hockey Writers Association to the player who "best exemplifies the qualities of perseverance, sportsmanship, and dedication to ice hockey." Which frequently means the player who overcame the most horrific injury, illness, or personal strife. Or, worst of all, old age.

The Michigan: The "lacrosse goal" first popularized by Mike Legg at the University of Michigan, in which the attacking player lifts the puck on his stick blade and scores high over the goalie's shoulder. A YouTube favorite.

Mitts: Double meaning! Mitts can refer to a player's hands, which are frequently called "filthy" or "silky." Mitts can also refer to the gloves that cover those hands, which are dropped to fight.

Natural Hat Trick: When a player scores three goals in a row, uninterrupted by another goal. Also, a hat trick without any artificial flavors or preservatives.

Norris Trophy: Given by the Professional Hockey Writers Association to the defenseman who "demonstrates throughout the season the greatest all-round ability in the position," which often means "most points" and "most fame" and "sometimes, actual defense optional."

Offer Sheets: An offer made by a team to a restricted free agent, which can then be matched by the team holding his rights. If it is, then the team signing the player must give a compensation package to the team losing the player. This probably sounds very interesting and exciting, but unfortunately the NHL is an old-boys network in which the teams have basically agreed not to traffic in these dark arts, despite their obvious path to quick team rebuilding.

One-Timer: Immediately shooting the puck after receiving a pass. Usually accompanied by the words "wicked," "nasty," or "whiffed on a."

PDO: A stat that measures shooting percentage plus save percentage, and indicates whether a team is having good or bad "puck luck."

Penalty Shot: Awarded to a player for several reasons—from a scoring chance being denied by a penalty on a breakaway to a non-goalie covering the puck in the defensive goal crease—it's one of the most exciting plays in hockey when it isn't being completely watered down by overtime skills competitions.

Players-Only Meeting: The thing that happens when a team's fortunes hit rock bottom and/or right before its coach is unemployed.

Poke-Check: A play in which one uses his stick to knock a puck off an opponent's stick. Typically used by a goalie.

"Potvin Sucks": An endearing chant heard echoing through Madison Square Garden, as Rangers fans honor Islanders Hall of Famer Denis Potvin with this own special endorsement of his skills. Its tune is whistled for three bars before the chorus chimes in. Co-opted by New Jersey Devils fans and turned into the equally creative and effective "Rangers Suck."

Plus/Minus: Much-maligned stat that indicates which players are on the ice for a goal, but essentially tells us nothing.

Prince of Wales Trophy: The award given to the Eastern Conference champion, which was formerly given to the Wales Conference champion, before the NHL changed the names of all the conferences and divisions because they think American fans are idiots.

Puck Bunny: A term that was used to describe groupies that was regrettably turned into a blanket label for all women who follow hockey. It's an insulting pejorative that should be removed from the societal lexicon, so let's do that, shall we?

Puck over the Glass: When a defensive player in his own zone puts the puck over the glass in any part of the rink, a delay-of-game penalty is assessed. Originally, this was supposed to be a subjective call by the referees, but they're just way too busy to worry about that crap and just call it every time.

Puttin' on the Foil: A metaphor for fighting, as inspired by the Hanson Brothers literally wrapping their hands in foil before a game in *Slap Shot*.

Pylon: An extraordinarily slow skater and a defensive liability who allows offensive players to skate around him like they're controlling the puck through a stick-handling drill.

Restricted Free Agent (RFA): A player who is still in indentured servitude to his NHL team. Players only become unrestricted free agents when they turn 27 or have upwards of seven years in the league. RFAs receive qualifying offers from teams to retain their rights; if one isn't made, they go UFA. Players and teams can also use salary arbitration as a way to remedy salary disputes.

Rocket Richard Trophy: Given to the player who scored the most goals in the regular season. Meanwhile, Players with the Most Assists is given the equally prestigious "pays the bar tab for the Rocket Richard winner."

Roughing: Defined as "a punching motion with the hand or fist, with or without the glove on the hand, normally directed at the head or face of an opponent." In actuality, an excuse to take one player from each team to the penalty box to hand everyone else on the ice a chill pill.

Rule 48: Established in 2010, this rule banned "targeted hits to the head from the lateral or blind side" after a series of catastrophic hits in the preceding year. It was later changed to a hit to "an opponent's head where the head was the main point of contact and such contact to the head was avoidable." The punishment: a minor penalty or a match penalty for an intentional hit to the head.

Sauce: The amount of power one puts behind a shot or pass. Sometimes players get a bit more specific and call it "mustard."

Saucer Pass: A pass that flies off the ice and travels stick to stick, traveling through the air like a flying saucer. Many of these passes have yet to be declassified by the U.S. military.

Selke Trophy: Given by the Professional Hockey Writers Association to the player "who demonstrates the most skill in the defensive component of the game," which usually boils down to an inane formula of faceoff wins and shorthanded ice time by voters.

Shinny: An informal game of pond or street hockey, it's a term used to describe an NHL game that lacks form, structure, or competent defense.

Sieve: A goalie who allows the puck to pass through him like water through a sieve.

Sin Bin: The penalty box. As they said in *Slap Shot*, you go there and feel shame.

"Skinny Medium Fat Fat": The most popular configuration of players on Nintendo *Ice Hockey*, and a reference you can drop if you really want to impress your friends over the age of 40.

***Slap Shot*:** Seriously, just watch the movie if you haven't. Or if you have, watch it again.

Slashing: When a player swings his stick at an opponent. Normally, a tap on the gloves or the stick wouldn't be slashing. But since everyone drops his stick like it spontaneously combusted the moment they feel a stick anywhere near their gloves, it usually is.

Slew Foot: Kicking out an opponent's skates while forcing them down to the ice, in one of the most heinous and frowned upon acts in hockey.

Snipe: A pinpoint shot that beats a goalie.

Spearing: Stabbing an opponent with the point of the stick blade. It earns a double-minor penalty for an attempt and a major for a successful one, which carries a game misconduct. Also known as "harpooning" until the Hartford Whalers relocated to Raleigh.

Spengler Cup: An annual invitation tournament held in Davos, Switzerland, that's open to both league clubs and national teams. It is not named for Dr. Egon Spengler, a collector of spores, molds, and fungus.

Stanley Cup: The Holy Grail. Also, it's been pooped in by a baby.

Ted Lindsay Award: Given by the NHL Players Association to the "most outstanding player in the regular season." It's an actual Player of the Year award, while the Hart Trophy is only voted on like it's one.

Toe Drag: A deke move in which the puck is pushed forward before being dragged back with the end (i.e., the toe) of the stick blade.

Trapper: Another name for the goalie's glove, and also the occupation for 90 percent of Canadian players had hockey not worked out.

Tripping: When a player uses the stick, knee, foot, arm, hand, or elbow to cause his opponent to trip or fall. Also, what general managers "be doin'" when handing out long-term contracts to goalies.

Turning Your Back to the Play: When a player attempts to draw a penalty by turning his numbers to an onrushing checker. Which is as dangerous as it sounds.

Twig: Despite none of them actually being made of wood any longer, another name for a stick.

Vezina Trophy: Given to the goalie "adjudged to be the best at this position" by the NHL's general managers, the same guys who criminally overrate and overpay goalies every season.

Waffle-Boarded: A save with the blocker, as called by announcer Mike "Doc" Emrick.

War Room: The NHL's video review center in Toronto, where controversial goal calls are confirmed or denied after a group of execs analyze the tape.

Whale, The: The single most beloved franchise in NHL history, from its blue-collar home in Hartford to "Brass Bonanza," the greatest goal song ever. Also the single most glaring example of absence making the heart grow fonder.

Worlds: Shorthand for the IIHF World Championships, an annual tournament that's enormously important to everyone but Americans, considering that we haven't won gold in it since 1933 and because it's quite obviously the NIT to the Stanley Cup Playoffs' March Madness.

World Juniors: Shorthand for the IIHF Under-20 World Junior Championships, an annual tournament that exists as affirmation of Canada's hockey dominance or a reason for Canada to question its entire player development program in the inconceivable event it loses.

WOWY: The "With or Without You" stats that show how a player has fared competing with a teammate, playing without that teammate, and how the team reacts when they're on or off the ice.

Zamboni: A popular brand of ice-resurfacing machine. Please remember all ice-resurfacing machines aren't Zambonis but all Zambonis are ice-resurfacing machines. Well, except the Canadian rock band The Zambonis. We imagine it'd take them a while to resurface the ice. And we'd rather not know how.

Zone-Adjusted Stats: Stats that remove the 10 seconds immediately after a zone faceoff; according to Puckalytics, "It has been shown that the majority of the benefit or penalty of a zone start occurs during the first 10 seconds."

Zone Starts: In which zones did the player start the majority of his shifts during the game? This stat gives a percentage. It's a handy way to determine which star players are doing the "heavy lifting" to put up points…and which players are being protected from being defensive liabilities by their coaches.

Zyuzin, Andrei: A defenseman who played from 1997 to 2008 in the NHL, and alphabetically the last name listed among all the players who ever saw even a minute in the NHL. And now you can win that bar bet.

CHAPTER 14

THE FUTURE

Few saw it as an innovation.

Many viewed it as a detriment to the game: a way to embarrass defensemen, a way to confuse fans, a way to make players exhausted husks by night's end.

"It is an *absurd* rule," trumpeted the *Toronto Daily Star*, "as the teams will discover as the season progresses."

The year was 1913. Lester and Frank Patrick had allowed the first forward passes in professional hockey in the Pacific Coast Hockey League—only at center ice, between these new blue lines they put down in the rink. Many critics saw it as heresy and a negative change for the game. Over the next century, we'd see how fundamentally wrong they were, as the forward pass birthed the game we see today.

But they weren't fundamentally wrong for their time. You see, back in those days, players tried to play the entire game, refusing to come off the ice for a sub. Author Craig Bowlsby chronicled how a 1919 championship series between Montreal and Seattle featured an overtime game that sent several players to the hospital, their bodies ravaged by fatigue and H1N1 influenza. Hall of Famer Joe Hall died during the 1919 Stanley Cup Final because of it, and from that point the hockey world began working on adding more players to the roster, which eventually led to rolling line changes during a game.

Which, again, were a thing more than a century ago.

We might never see another fundamental change to the game on that level—maybe if they ever dropped even strength to 4-on-4 or, like, added a second goalie to the crease to guard a soccer-sized net. But hockey is an ever-changing sport, from the gear to the way we watch on television.

What does the future hold?

INFORMATION OVERLOAD

The NHL has seen a stats revolution over the last decade, as fan-created metrics measured things like puck possession, shooting percentage, and quality of competition like never before. Marginal players were reconsidered as important supporting cast members thanks to the way these advanced stats quantified their worth. Star players were now measured beyond their sexiest offensive stats. Media members were forced to do more than just look at faceoff percentage when voting on the Selke.

But ultimately the numbers are projections, based on the number of shots taken and attempted by opponents. They don't tell us actual puck-on-stick possession, and they don't tell us much about the shots themselves. They're important projections, to be sure, but ultimately it's data scraped from a play-by-play document created by human scorers.

The first steps to change that were taken in January 2015, when the NHL tested player-tracked technology during the All-Star Game. A chip was placed in a pocket inside the back of a player's jersey, an infrared sensor. Infrared emitters were embedded inside and around a puck. Cameras were placed around the rink to collect the data given off by the puck and the players, each of whom had his own unique signature.

Sportvision, the company that added digital enhancement to any number of sports broadcasts, found a way to do what the NHL has tried to do for years—put a chip in the puck without fundamentally changing it.

Oh, the NHL tried. Trouble is that the puck's weight would increase too much, or the puck would split apart when smacked with a stick blade.

"Our puck uses infrared emitters, what we call active tracking," said Sportvision CEO Hank Adams. They use the same technology in the NBA and for NASCAR. The problem with the NHL, he said, is that there are too many collisions to simply track the players. They had to put sensors on the actual puck, along with sensors inside the collars of the players' jerseys.

"There's a chip in the puck, and infrared lights are shined through these light tubes," he said. "We have infrared cameras up in the catwalks, 10 of them. They see the flash of the puck, which is a unique frequency, and different than the flash of a player tag. And each player tag has a different frequency. We slip it into a pocket of the jersey, and it shines through brightly."

The important thing about the puck was that it wasn't fundamentally changed. Adams said the puck acts the same way as a regulation puck, despite having four emitters on top and bottom, as well as 10 around the outside of puck.

The data collected by this tech is redefining. Everything about a shot—time of possession, position on the ice, release time, velocity of the shot, angle of the shot, how and when a goalie reacts, the position of the other players when the shot is taken—can be measured in real time, which means it can be delivered live on a TV broadcast or in a second-screen experience.

The data collected will pinpoint metrics like puck possession and time on ice. It would also capture information about shot speed and skating speed like never before, delivering that information in real time. It will also paint a full picture of every shot on goal in the game.

"For shots on goal, there's an official definition: will it have gone in if not for the goalie? Well, we know where the puck is, we know how far away the goal is. And there are things we can automate, like if the puck was deflected by a stick above the crossbar," said Adams.

It's a data explosion for the NHL.

"In short, we are attempting to embark upon a journey that hopefully will enable us to create and then maintain a digital record of everything in our game and compile a complete digital history," said NHL commissioner Gary Bettman.

He's not kidding: this technology allows the NHL to digitally re-create any game situation in a 3-D format. Consider a scoring play; now imagine if you could swoop through it like a camera on a drone, seeing what every player is doing during the play.

Think about EA Sports' NHL series. Now imagine actual games presented in that environment. Rewind plays. Pause them. Parse them. Analyze them. You can see past the eyes of players.

Furthermore, you could actually *become the puck* and follow the play from stick to stick until "you" fly past the goalie and cross the goal line.

But that's not the only revolutionary view the NHL wants to serve up.

NEW REALITY TV

The NHL has always struggled to crack the code on television. You've heard all the complaints: it's impossible to see all the players all of the time. It's sometimes difficult to track the puck. Yadda yadda yadda.

The league tried innovations like the much-hated glow puck—which I named one of the top 10 worst ideas in sports history in a previous book—that were disasters. Then came the advent of HDTV, which helped: the clear picture and letterbox format allowed fans to see more of the ice and better see the puck.

But even with surround sound in your man (or woman) cave, the in-arena reality was something television could never duplicate.

Which is why the NHL and other leagues are headed to a new reality.

In 2015, the league tested cameras that could create a 360-degree live-streaming virtual reality experience for users wearing special VR headsets.

Imagine if NHL games were no longer confined to the gaze of the big swinging camera at the red line. You could choose a virtual seat behind the nets or in the corners and watch the game from that perspective. You would also have the ability to automatically change your perspective on a play. One test the NHL ran at the Stadium Series allowed viewers to go from a perspective in the stands to one directly above the goalie and the goal line.

Picture this: you try to get tickets to a Stanley Cup Final game at your local arena, in your favorite seats. You fail, as it's sold out. So, instead, you settle into your well-worn couch to watch the game at home...from your favorite seats at the arena, through the virtual reality gear strapped to you. You're immersed in a live, 360-degree environment that does everything but allow you to buy cotton candy from that vendor walking down the stairs.

"It was wild. I could turn around and see a person sitting in back of me," said NHL COO John Collins, who strapped on the goggles to watch footage of the NHL Stadium Series game in Santa Clara. "There's going to be a technology soon where you're going to be sitting at home and pick where you want to watch the game. You could be sitting at home and still watch it from your seat."

Now, VR isn't exactly an easy sell. How many times have you walked past an arcade at an amusement park or on the boardwalk and seen that

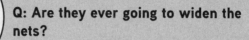

Q: Are they ever going to widen the nets?

A: Over Roberto Luongo's dead body they will!

"I've been working 20 years at a game I love trying to improve myself, and to start over from square one is not something I'm interested in," Luongo said back in 2009 on the prospect of widening the nets. "It changes everything for the goalie and it doesn't, in my mind, bring more excitement to the game if the nets are bigger and guys score from the blue line."

We won't see soccer-style-wide nets for that reason. Despite the siren's song of increased goal-scoring, it would be too radical a change.

What about something a little less revolutionary?

Goalie coach François Allaire had an idea some time ago: the goal cage remains six feet wide and four feet high, but instead of circular posts, the net has oval-shaped posts with the flatter, longer side positioned on the inside of the goal. Think parentheses.

The thought was that pucks that previously bounced off the posts would have a better chance of sneaking in or bouncing in off the iron.

$20 per game virtual reality pen standing empty? It's already been a task to get people to wear 3-D glasses in their homes; is there any chance they'll wear VR headsets?

That's where the real innovation lies: in theory, the VR experience will be streamed to your phone, which you would wear on a lightweight headset. No bulky new tech, just the tech you already have in your pocket.

The question many ask about virtual reality: will it eventually replace the game-going experience?

"I don't have any official stats, but I would say one out of every four shots that beat a goalie but hit the inside of the post bounces in rather than straight out," Allaire said. "If we can cut the posts in half and have a flat surface turned inward, you would see more goals. This would make the net bigger by about two inches on the width and an inch on the height.... It would not take away from the skill of a goaltender, but would reward the shooter for beating the goalie."

Mitch Korn, the legendary goalie coach, also made a proposal years ago to increase the size of the net—by height, rather than by width.

"If you make the nets wider, you fundamentally change the way goalies play the position. All the instincts. All that stuff," he said. "If you make them higher, all the saves goalies make just because they're big, you can score. And if they have to protect the top of the net in case the puck is elevated, well, guess what: they're going to have to stand up more, and that means the bottom of the net will be exposed."

So there's only a chance the nets are widened one day, if scoring decreases and there's a clamor for it. But if they ever do, clearly they should ask a goalie coach to design it...

Allen says the social aspect of the arena experience can't be replaced, which is true: while home theaters, man caves, and readily available (legal and illegal) streaming of games is always at the ready, the best one can hope for as far as the social aspect translating to home viewing is having a running stream of tweets, comments, and Facebook activities on a second screen.

There really is no replacing that moment when a goal is scored, and you're bear hugging a stranger next to you while trying not to spill your beer. Or pouring your beer on him because he's cheering for the wrong team, and getting a bear hug from security.

THE NEW GEAR

The motivations for gear innovations are driven by two factors: player safety and customization. Craig Desjardins, general manager for Bauer Hockey, sees both shaping how hockey equipment is manufactured and developed.

From a player-safety perspective, the R&D for Bauer and other hockey gear companies is centered around energy transfers—how much energy is being passed from one player to another on a hit, and how much energy is being absorbed by the hittee. The more they learn, the more they can apply new materials and approaches to make players safer—finding pads that fit closer to the body and using lighter weight materials for all protective gear, for example.

Have these companies exhausted their materials innovation? In some ways, yes. There are only so many ways you can build a composite stick. So for Bauer, the solution isn't found on the ice but in the air. "We're working with composite suppliers who are working with Boeing and Airbus on initiatives that are beyond anything that is being done in sporting goods today," said Desjardins.

Hey, if the materials can make a plane fly faster without sacrificing safety, perhaps they can do the same for a skater.

Those skaters, meanwhile, are like snowflakes in the eyes of gear makers: every one is unique. And cold and wet.

So the task for companies like Bauer Hockey is to customize gear, from helmets to skates, to the specifications of the players. Not just in their height and weight—that's the easy stuff—but in how they play the game.

Think of a Formula One driver. His car is fitted for him, customized to his needs, and not the other way around. So when it comes to a player's skate, it's not just the weight of the materials and the protection it provides, but whether the build of the thing matches a player's skating stride. Do they have a deep knee bend? Do they take three hard strides and then glide? The skate will be made to compensate for that.

Goaltending gear is already more customizable than that of skaters, and the trend will continue. Pads will become increasingly lighter—by almost 30 percent—allowing netminders to have greater stamina late in games.

But Mitch Korn, the goalie guru for the Washington Capitals, sees another more revolutionary innovation on the horizon.

"Here's what's going to happen, and the NHLPA is going to fight it until the cows come home. They're going to have a body suit. You're going to be able to go into this body suit which will protect your arms and your torso, probably right down to your knees—without hockey pads. Up until the goalie pads," he said.

(Don't worry, hockey significant others: they'll still likely wear a cup.)

"It's going to be made of a gel that can absorb pucks. You'll never feel it. The technology is there," said Korn.

So mask, blocker, glove, stick, and goalie pads, and the rest is the speedskater-like gel body suit.

"You ask me how it's going to be different? I think the body protection is going to be enormous," said Korn.

Of course, the most significant material change for the NHL and its gear has nothing to do with player safety or improved performance… unless it's the improved performance of the NHL to its shareholders.

Ads on jerseys. They'll be here within five years. The only things we can pray for are that NHL sweaters don't become the NASCAR drivers-on-acid jerseys from European leagues, that the NHL continues to sell ad-free jerseys to its fans, and that some team is bold enough to take a jersey ad from a sexual enhancement and/or feminine hygiene product.

THE GAME ITSELF

Where will the NHL's gameplay go over the next 10 years?

Every major change in the NHL's rules is driven by one of two things: player safety or scoring.

If scoring is down thanks to defensive systems and incredible goaltending, the first attack will always be against the systems. That's the way it went back in 2005, when the NHL decided to "take out the red line" and legalize two-line passes.

Hurray, they said, *long stretch passes will mean the death of defensive trapping and the creativity-stifling systems that have turned our most glorious game into a chess match, if each piece moved with a cast-iron anchor tied around its base.*

For the most part, this was true: home-run passes through the neutral zone were no longer whistled down, leading to thrilling breakaways that cut through the defensive systems.

Alas, what the removal of the red line also did was sap some of the offensive creativity from the game: teams forego skating through the neutral zone to set up plays and instead send the puck from their own zone to the opposing blue line, where it is chipped into the zone. This now happens roughly once every 90 seconds, which can be super boring.

So there's a chance the red line could return in the next several years. Or, perhaps, there's a way to keep two-line passes but make it more difficult for teams to just send the puck down the ice all willy-nilly.

One innovation championed by no less an authority than Scotty Bowman: the Ringette Line.

Ringette is a Canadian game played on ice that uses straight sticks and a blue rubber ring, and the Ringette Line marks off the restricted area of a team's defending zone. But in Bowman's vision for the NHL, the line would be painted across the ice at the top of the faceoff circles in each zone. The team that has the puck would need to gain the ringette line to make a legal pass through the red line at center ice. Any pass that originates behind the ringette line and connects over the red line would be illegal.

What would it do to the game? Well, in theory, it would cause more opportunities for forechecking teams to force a turnover in the attacking zone as players would no longer be able to simply hammer the puck along the boards.

The rule was debated in 2013, and didn't garner enough support for implementation.

Forcing teams to make plays with the puck rather than just hammer it around the ice is something many general managers and league officials have argued for during rules debates.

For example, the NHL's Research and Development Camp of 2011 looked at a new rule for the penalty kill that would force defensive players to skate the puck over their own blue line instead of (legally) icing the puck. This would ratchet up the pressure on teams in their own zone, tiring out penalty-killers and creating more chances.

Lou Lamoriello, now the general manager of the Toronto Maple Leafs, has lobbied for a more dramatic change to the penalty kill: going back to the halcyon days of the "two-minute major," i.e., score as many goals as one can on the power play even if it's a minor penalty. This used to be the way things were done in the NHL, until the Montreal Canadiens of Rocket Richard would, like, score *all the goals*.

(Another ancillary benefit of the rule: perhaps teams would think twice about taking stupid penalties if it meant two minutes of power-play time that would be the hockey equivalent of Super Mario grabbing a star and running through turtles and mushrooms.)

How else to increase scoring?

How about just letting the players kick the puck into the net? Look, the "no kicking" rule was adopted back in the day when goalies didn't wear masks and 100 pounds of padding. And every season, there are a few dozen goals that are disqualified because the player used a "distinct kicking motion," which usually means using his leg like a pendulum. Literally every other puck off the skates is counted when it crosses the line—would it be all that outlandish to see "distinct" kicks earn the same pass?

What about faceoffs? There's been a thought that cheaters on draws should be punished more harshly. One notion, also from the R&D Camp: "If a player is deemed to have committed a faceoff violation, he will be required to move back and keep his skates behind a 'penalty line' (one foot farther back) which will cause a loss of leverage and therefore loss of strength for the ensuing faceoff."

Another idea kicked around for years is that of the "set puck." The linesman would place the puck on the dot. The players would come set. The linesman would blow his whistle, pick up the puck, and then drop it.

Well, what if we eliminate the need for a linesman to drop it, seeing as how puck drops are woefully inconsistent? Another idea had the puck set in place between the players, and then they battle for it when the whistle is blown, sans linesman drop.

Heck, why not go the full XFL and have two skaters charging at the puck at full speed, and whoever doesn't break his collarbone wins the draw?

Because player safety is why, and, as we said earlier, it's also a driving force behind rules changes. Think hits to the head, or hybrid icing.

The tug-of-war between hockey as a free-wheeling sport and one that puts an emphasis on player safety will continue for years.

In many ways, it's an argument about obstruction: how much of it do we want in the game? Because a little goes a long way: the 2005 rules changes created a virtual track meet in the NHL, with players rocketing down the ice and hitting each other at a high velocity, unencumbered. The idea that allowing some levels of obstruction to slow the game down has its champions, even if it means a slide toward the hockey we saw in the 1990s, which was sometimes unwatchable.

Morbid as this sounds, it's reality: no one wants to "take hitting out of the game," but it's entirely possible that some catastrophic injury will bring dramatic changes to the rules. A boarding penalty that results in paralysis. A charging penalty that results in something even worse.

One player-safety innovation championed by both Brian Burke and Pierre McGuire was the "bear hug rule," which is slightly less adorable than it sounds.

"What forwards have done in our league is they turn their backs on defensemen to protect the puck. It's a tactic. They're betting a defenseman won't finish his check and sometimes a defenseman does, where all their force goes into that player and all that force goes into the boards," said Burke. "They're taking risks that they shouldn't take. Especially when they turn back with the puck where the defenseman's on their ass and he's committed to the hit, that defenseman can't do anything there but finish his hit."

So Burke has lobbied for the "bear hug," in which the freight-train collisions along the boards between players would be replaced by an onrushing player wrapping his arms around his target as they skated to the boards.

It would be a leap forward for player safety, but the premise that NHL officials should be given yet another subjective rule to enforce is a frustrating one. It's legalized holding; good luck trying to parse how long is too long in the bear hug. ("No, seriously, Mr. Referee, it wasn't that I was holding him, it's that I think we really connected on

Q: Are they ever going to widen the ice?

A: It's a question asked every four years when fans watch the Olympic men's hockey tournament, when it's played on a European ice surface, and assume that level of hockey skill can be transplanted into the NHL if the arena rinks were just made wider.

Of course, that ignores the fact that we're watching a single-elimination tournament of all-star teams. And the NHL is...not that.

International Ice Hockey Federation ice is roughly 200 by 100 feet. "I think the Olympic size is too big," forward James van Riemsdyk told the *Toronto Star* in 2014. "But if there was five more feet [in NHL rinks], I think with how big guys are now and how fast guys are, that extra bit of room would be great. It doesn't completely alter the game. You've got that extra time where you can spread the defense out a little bit more. If you're trying to dodge a hit, you have a little bit of extra room to play with. It just creates more lanes to make more plays. But all the rinks are in, so it'd be tough to do that."

It would be, because wider ice means having to push the boards out into some very expensive real estate in the arena, taking away some of the most desirable seats in the place.

But as players get larger, the ice gets more crowded, and the game always needs to evolve, so the idea that the ice could be expanded by a few feet isn't outlandish.

A happy compromise: what if newer NHL arenas were built with larger ice surfaces, and the other arenas can figure out if that's where they want to go, too?

Hey, if baseball teams have to face the Green Monster in Fenway, why couldn't hockey teams face the Big Ice in Detroit?

a very masculine yet spiritual level and I didn't want him to escape my embrace…")

Another rule that's been considered is an innovation on the ice: the "warning track."

Thomas Smith spent 27 months in a wheelchair and remains partially paralyzed after being tripped into the boards when he was 20 years old. In 2014, he championed "The Look-Up Line": a 40-inch orange band along the boards that would help puck-carriers and the players who would hit them know they're in a dangerous area.

Think of it in baseball terms: an outfielder runs full-speed to catch a fly ball hit toward the center-field wall. Suddenly, the grass gives way to dirt under his feet, and the outfielder knows that if the brakes aren't applied, and if he can't phase through solid matter like Kitty Pryde of the X-Men, he's going splat against the wall.

A warning track for hockey would accomplish a few key things. It would warn players to keep their heads up to help avoid head and neck injuries. It would warn players to be careful not to check (contact) opposing players from behind. It would allow players time to make proper bodily adjustments before hitting the boards. It would alleviate the failure-to-warn (board-related) issue that currently exists in hockey.

Sure, it might look like a giant stripe of chewed-up Cheetos on the ice, but it could dramatically reduce injuries along the boards in the NHL, as it has in more than 230 rinks around the U.S. already.

It all comes back to player safety, which means it all comes back to concussions.

The NHL will continue to learn about concussions and their effects on athletes during their playing days and afterward.

Diagnoses could change dramatically. There are blood tests for concussions—which detect brain injuries through elevated levels of certain proteins—that could be used to rapidly determine if a player suffered one during the game.

This would be a giant leap forward for concussion testing, which currently relies on baseline testing. "Players are given a baseline test before the season starts. Those who really want to play tend to lowball their responses so there won't be a noticeable difference if they perform poorly after an injury," said biomedical engineer Damir Janigro, who has helped develop the concussion blood test.

"Point of care" blood tests are a ways away, but the early indications are promising.

THE NHL ITSELF

Expansion will happen; it's just a matter of how many teams the league adds and which markets it expands to. Just remember this fast and loose rule: the NHL loves expanding into no-sure-thing first-time markets and would love to keep the sure things (i.e., Canadian markets) in its back pocket in case some failing team needs to relocate.

Outdoor games will continue to happen. As we cycle through all of the large stadia in NHL markets, "neutral site" games will start to creep into the schedule. How about a Winter Classic at Lambeau Field?

So will non-traditional venues. How about a Rangers vs. Islanders game in Central Park? Or a hockey game played on some glacier in the Northern Territories?

For the time being, the NHL will try to limit the number of outdoor games each season. Could there be more? Better question: could the outdoor game gimmick be sustained if every team in the league had one outdoor game every season? Even the ones, like, in Florida?

The World Cup of Hockey is the first step for the NHL's European invasion. There will be Ryder Cup–style events in Europe. There will be regular-season games in Europe. There might even be an outdoor game somewhere in Europe on a Winter Classic scale.

Will there ever be an NHL Europe? Logistics would make it impossible to integrate Euro teams in the NHL regular season, but an NHL-branded league across Europe doesn't seem implausible, given the revenues on the table over there.

The makeup of the NHL will continue to become more diverse, both in geographic and cultural scope.

With teams in American non-traditional markets and millions spent on bringing hockey to places other than majority-white suburbs, the league is seeing real improvement in attracting a more diverse player and fan base.

"By giving kids access, they're starting to make some choices that they may want to participate in this sport," Ken Martin, the NHL's vice president of community affairs and diversity programming, told the *Buffalo News* in 2013. "It's such an important thing for these kids. I know my son who played hockey, he's 22 now, but when he was seven we used to go to tournaments and we were the only minority there. Now you go to all these tournaments and you see a wealth of minorities playing and participating in the game."

You'll see an NHL that's more socially conscious, both in the way minority players are treated and in determining if the sport is welcoming to women and minorities. We'll see the first openly gay player in the NHL in the next five years. You'll see a league making an attempt to prove that one of its advertising slogans—"Hockey is for everyone"—isn't just lip service.

And then, in 2020, we'll have another lockout, as the owners attempt to undo all of the long-term, high-priced boondoggle contracts on their rosters by shutting down part of the season.

It's never fun when someone forces you to take your eye off the puck.

But we're hockey fans.

We're used to it by now.

And we always come back...

=ACKNOWLEDGMENTS=

One of the greatest things about being a journalist is speaking with people who are far more knowledgeable than you are on a given subject in order to gather facts, create informed opinions, and generally not sound like a complete moron. Mostly.

To that end, a debt of thanks to those who imparted with some of that knowledge in these pages, including Dan Ages, Karl Alzner, Paul Bissonnette, Justin Bourne, John Collins, Ken Daneyko, Craig Desjardins, Zach Dinga, Kyle Dubas, Mike Johnson, Mitch Korn, Brad May, Jeff Marek, Eddie Olczyk, Brent Peterson, Brad Treliving, Barry Trotz, Aaron Ward, Kevin Weekes, Kevin Woodley, and many, many others. I'd also like to acknowledge the influence of *Hockey Plays and Strategies* by Mike Johnston and Ryan Walter, which has been a constant resource since its release and remains a great primer for new fans.

Thanks to my editor Adam Motin and the great folks at Triumph Books for their support and unbelievable patience. Thanks to the Yahoo! Sports family, and especially the hardest-working bloggers in the business at Puck Daddy, for their encouragement.

Finally, thanks to Rubie Edmondson for the inspiration and unbelievable support, Bob and Pat Wyshynski for infecting me with this particular strain of sports fandom, and Vivien Wyshynski for allowing me the chance to introduce that fanaticism to someone beautiful and brilliant.

=ABOUT THE AUTHOR=

Greg Wyshynski is an award-winning writer, blogger, and editor, best known for creating Yahoo! Sports' popular hockey blog, *Puck Daddy*. He was the executive sports editor for The Connection Newspapers chain in the Washington, D.C., area for nearly a decade, winning more than 50 Virginia Press Association awards. He was a featured writer on Deadspin and AOL Sports, and had his work appear in *The Hockey News*, where he was the first blogger ever named to its "100 People of Power and Influence" list. He co-hosts the popular *Marek* vs. *Wyshynski* hockey podcast, available on iTunes. His previous book was *Glow Pucks and 10-Cent Beer: The 101 Worst Ideas in Sports History*. He lives in New York City, uncomfortable as that is for a die-hard New Jersey Devils fan. Follow him on Twitter @wyshynski.